attitudes
1

*"He Sent Forth His Word and
Healed Them"* PSALMS 107:20

Virgil Leach

D1160808

QUALITY PUBLICATIONS
P O BOX 1060   ABILENE, TEXAS 79604

FOREWORD

It is fortunate when one has talent, but talent is cheap. You can buy it, people sell it; you can find it everywhere. But attitudes are not for sale. You can't buy an attitude for a million dollars. We are literally surrounded by talent. We see it in school, in business, in government, even in our own homes. Again it is everywhere! But we are also aware that there are millions of talented alcoholics. There is no way to compare talents with attitudes.

Not only is talent cheap, so is education. You can get it. It is available everywhere. Most anyone can receive a degree or even a whole string of them if he wants to. But let us remember there are millions of educated derelicts. There is no way to compare education with attitudes.

Also we find all around us an abundance of aptitude. It is also cheap. But again attitudes are just not for sale. How wonderful it would be if every teacher would pass on attitudes as the one great thing to be gained for our young people.

It is not so much what a person knows or is able to do or possess but rather the question is what kind of person am I. Perhaps all of us have witnessed only too often an ugly spirit or attitude that has brought great harm. A bad attitude can spoil almost any situation. On the other hand, a good attitude can enhance, or make right almost any adverse condition that may exist.

The Value Of This Manual

Just ask mothers and fathers all over our country; they will tell you what their children need. They will immediately affirm that this material is vital, needed, and gets specifically to the point. Question every employer, schoolteacher, elder, judge, statesman or those from a broken home; in every case they will reply the same. This book contains a simple, sincere, understandable code for training youth that will prepare them for the future that lies so precariously before them. It will have its effect on them in a positive way and be of eternal worth.

Careful and skillful hands have gathered the best possible material. Its practical value rests on the fact that it may be used in the church, the home, and in connection with any of the plans you may have for the development of your young people.

Training youth is our most important responsibility. It should come before all else. This manual presents a new and refreshing approach to getting the job done. The lessons are superior and will guard against the pitfalls of life. Each lesson gets to the heart and soul of developing Christian characteristics, and presents standards we've always hoped to achieve in our sons and daughters. It gives complete analysis of attitudes vital to every living person and how to develop them. We must remember that our number one problem everywhere is attitude.

The commentary, the Scripture back-up, questions and assignments leave an unforgettable impression, and will bless the student and teacher alike. It will be a pleasure to teach. Our whole aim is to fashion lives into the image and likeness of the Savior who grew in wisdom and stature, and in favor with God and man. Each lesson is in touch with life's realities, deals with daily needs, and will become a bulwark of strength to enable them to be all they should be in the home, school, marriage, church, or whatever vocation they might choose in life.

Perhaps in the past we have been too vague and general in presenting the ideals of proper attitudes, responsibility and Christian character. We believe that it would be well for every teacher, regardless of what age group being taught, to have this material in their hands, even if used no more than a supplement to their class. Let it be at their fingertips as a constant companion, counselor, and co-worker. It will equip them to see more clearly what the real aim of their class should be, and will be a gage to spiritual maturity.

ATTITUDES 1 includes 26 valuable attitude lessons, enough for a six-month study. **ATTITUDES 2** is also available for a continuing study of attitudes.

This entire book is designed for Teachers Manual. Should Student Workbook be desired, use only exercises with blanks and fill-in Scriptures plus the suggested assignments. Use Revised Standard Version except where King James Version is specified.

TABLE OF CONTENTS

Attitude Game Board

Attitude games have many options; of course it is wise first to have several lessons on attitudes before using attitude games. The game not only provides an interesting and exciting diversion but also makes learning fun.

One may use attitude games in learning centers to test how much students have grasped or retained from the teachers lessons. At the same time, it provides a technique of learning how to apply scriptures and interpret them in their true light. This is an urgent need.

One may have contests with as few as two students or as many as 30 depending on the occasion or size of the class. For example, all the boys may compete with all the girls. This can be done when the teacher reads a particular scripture holding it up before the class. The teacher then asks for a show of hands to see who knows where the scripture applies and to what particular attitude. The teacher alternates between boys and girls. Each side takes their respective turn to answer. The side that gets the most correct wins.

When only two or four compete with each other, all scriptures should be placed in a container. Each contestant in turn reaches into the container to draw out one scripture at a time which he places on proper square of the atttitude board. Use a watch or a three minute sand glass to see who can place the most scriptures on proper setting in the least amount of time.

Another option: the instructor can use the board as a review for students. Give each student a sheet of paper and have him write down the proper attitudes as teacher reads the scripture.

The Attitude Game is made of wood and the scriptures are placed on the removable circular rings. These rings have small punched out holes which enable them to be fastened to the nails on the board (see figure 1).

Attitude Boards can be made with less expense and work by using poster board for both the rings and board.

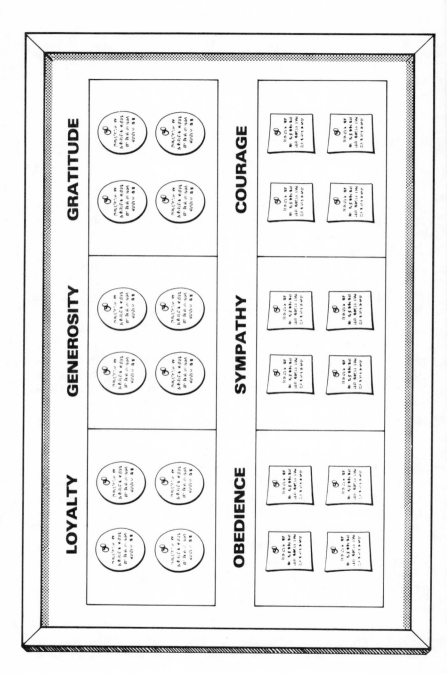

8

ATTITUDES
TEACHER'S CHECK LIST

LOYALTY

Philippians 3:8
Philippians 2:30
Matthew 16:24
Acts 21:13

OBEDIENCE

Hebrews 10:26
Matthew 7:21
Proverbs 1:24
Ephesians 6:2-3

TEMPER

Ephesians 4:26
Ecclesiastes 7:9
Matthew 5:22
1 John 2:11

GENEROSITY

John 3:16
Acts 20:35
Luke 19:8
2 Corinthians 9:7

SYMPATHY

Proverbs 21:13
Romans 12:15
1 Corinthians 12:26
Hebrews 4:5

COURAGE

Philippians 4:13
Isaiah 40:29
Joshua 1:5,6
Numbers 13:33

GRATITUDE

1 Timothy 4:4
Psalms 150:6
Romans 1:21
Malachi 2:2

MORALITY

Romans 1:24
Hebrews 13:4
Galatians 5:19
2 Timothy 2:22

GOOD SPEECH

1 Peter 3:10
Matthew 12:36
Proverbs 17:7
Proverbs 18:21

TRUTHFULNESS

Proverbs 19:9
Proverbs 6:16
Psalms 101:7
Acts 5:3

KINDNESS

Romans 12:20
Ephesians 4:32
Matthew 5:44
Luke 6:35

AMBITION

Proverbs 18:9
2 Chronicles 31:21
2 Thess. 3:10
1 Corithians 15:58

AIM HIGH

"Make no little plans: They have no magic to stir men's blood and probably themselves will not be realized. Make big plans: Aim high in hope and work, remembering that a noble, logical diagram once recorded will never die, but long after we are gone will be a living thing; asserting itself with ever growing insistency. Remember that our sons and grandsons are going to do things that would stagger us."

—Daniel Burnham

Cooperation

We read in Ecclesiastes 4:9-10, "Two are better than one, because they have a good reward for their toil. For if they fall, one will lift up his fellow; but woe to him that is alone when he falls and has not another to lift him up." Cooperation is the act of working jointly together for the same end; a mutual or common endeavor.

Joint action with others has made progress possible. If each of us had to produce his own food, make his own clothing, build his own house, and supply directly all of his other needs, we would find ourselves lacking in most of the conveniences with which our modern civilization is blessed. Union of effort makes many things possible that could not otherwise be attained, and is worth much more than the same amount of effort not united. For example, there might be some object too heavy for any one person to lift that would prove simple for two or more people to carry. Marcus Aurelius, the Roman emperor, regarded as representing the perfect ideal of the highest pre-Christian conception of character, said, "We are made for co-operation, like feet, like hands, like eyelids, like the rows of the upper and lower teeth. To act against one another then is contrary to Nature, and it is acting against one another to be vexed and turn away."

To the Corinthians the apostle Paul wrote, "I appeal to you, brethren, by the name of our Lord Jesus Christ, that all of you agree and that there be no dissensions among you, but that you be united in the same mind and the same judgment" (1 Corinthians 1:10). "For when one says, 'I belong to Paul,' and another 'I belong to Apollos,' are you not merely men? What then is Apollos? What is Paul? Servants through whom you believed, as the Lord assigned to each. I planted, Apollos watered, but God gave the growth. . . He

11

who plants and he who waters are equal, and each shall receive his wages according to his labor. For we are fellow workers for God; you are God's field, God's building. According to the commission of God given to me, like a skilled master builder I laid a foundation, and another man is building upon it" (1 Corinthians 3:4-10).

God would have us cooperate with one another in every way possible, thereby increasing the fruit of our labors, and also increasing our regard for one another. In James 5:16 we read, "Confess your sins to one another, and pray for one another, that you may be healed."

Paul wrote to the Corinthians, "Now there are varieties of gifts, but the same Spirit; and there are varieties of service, but the same Lord; and there are varieties of working, but it is the same God who inspires them all in every one. To each is given the manifestation of the Spirit for the common good. . . For just as the body is one and has many members, and all the members of the body, though many, are one body, so it is with Christ. For by one Spirit we were all baptized into one body. . . For the body does not consist of one member but of many. . . If all were a single organ, where would the body be? As it is, there are many parts, yet on body . . . God has so adjusted the body, giving the greater honor to the inferior part, that there may be no discord in the body, but that the members may have the same care for one another. If one member suffers, all suffer together; if one member is honored, all rejoice together" (1 Corinthians 12:4-26). Here then, we see the perfect example of cooperation. The very nature of the church calls for the individual members to work jointly together for the same end or purpose. Since cooperation is so vital, both in the spiritual and the temporal realms, each of us should do our best to work considerately and harmoniously with our associates whenever a united effort is needed.

Fill in Scriptures

1. _____Two are better than one, because they have a good reward for their toil. For if they fall, one will lift up his fellow.

2. _____I planted, Apollos watered, but God gave the growth.

3. _____When our enemies heard that it was known to us and that God had frustrated their plan, we all returned to the wall, each to his work. From that day on, half of my

servants worked on construction, and half held the spears, shields, bows, and coats of mail . . . Those who carried burdens were laden in such a way that each with one hand labored on the work and with the other held his weapon.

4._____Working together with him, then, we entreat you not to accept the grace of God in vain.

5._____For just as the body in one and has many members, and all the members of the body, though many, are one body.

6._____I appeal to you, brethren, by the name of our Lord Jesus Christ, that all of you agree and that there be no dissensions among you, but that you be united in the same mind and the same judgment.

7._____Can two walk together, except they be agreed?

8._____And all who believed were together and had all things in common.

9._____It is not good that man be alone; I will make him a helper.

10._____For Macedonia and Achaia have been pleased to make some contribution for the poor among the saints at Jerusalem; they were pleased to do it, and indeed they are in debt to them, for if the Gentiles have come to share in their spiritual blessings, they ought also to be of service to them in material blessings.

11._____Those who believed were of one heart and soul.

12._____Bear one another's burdens, and so fulfill the law of Christ.

13._____You also must help us by prayer.

Galatians 6:2	Acts 4:32	Ecclesiastes 4:9,10
2 Corinthians 1:11	Amos 3:3 KJV	Acts 2:44
1 Corinthians 3:6	1 Corinthians 12:12	1 Corinthians 1:10
Nehemiah 4:15-17	Genesis 2:18	2 Corinthians 6:1
Romans 15:26,27		

Questions for Discussion

1. Define cooperation.
2. Do you have a willingness and ability to work with others for

the advancement of Christ's cause?

3. Why is it that some can work quite well independently but not in a group?

4. How can selfishness, words, feelings and opinions spoil a united effort?

5. Name some programs that require a united effort for real success.

6. How is the church like a physical body?

7. If we can't work together in this world is there hope that we can in the next?

8. What can be done to build a spirit of unity and whole-hearted cooperation?

9. Should not the church have the best spirit of cooperation, the best supported programs, the best attendance, the best singing, the best advertising? Should we not strive for the best in everything?

10. Summarize the need, blessings, and rewards of full cooperation.

Suggested Assignments

1. Memorize Ecclesiastes 4:9 and Acts 2:44.

2. Make sentences of the following words: harmony; cooperation; together; unity.

Patience

"We exhort you, brethren, admonish the idle, encourage the faint-hearted, help the weak, be patient with them all" (1Thess. 5:14).

Patience is defined as the quality of suffering without complaint; endurance and perseverance; forbearance; fortitude.

Patience bears the troubles of life, great or small, without grumbling or complaining in looks, manner, or speech. Endurance bears suffering and hardship with determined firmness. Patience is the outgrowth of mind and soul; endurance requires physical stamina as well. Fortitude combines high courage with the habit and power of endurance; we face periods of unrelieved pain, or stretches of adversity with fortitude. Forbearance consists in refraining from a justly provoked action; it does not repay insult or injury in return. Each of these is an integral part of the virtue called "patience."

The Bible contains many exhortations to patience and examples of individuals who were patient. Job is, perhaps, the most outstanding example of patience in man that has ever been recorded.

We must endeavor to make this virtue a part of our character because it is the Lord's will that we be patient, and it is only by his patience that we exist today. We read in 2 Peter 3:9, "The Lord is not slack concerning his promise, as some men count slackness; but is long-suffering to us-ward, not willing that any should perish, but that all should come to repentance" (KJV). The apostle Paul says that patience is one of the fruits of the spirit (Galatians 5:22).

James, the Lord's brother, wrote Christians to "Be patient, therefore, brethren until the coming of the Lord. Behold, the farmer waits for the precious fruit of the earth, being patient over it until it receives the early and the late rain. You also be patient" (James 5:7,8).

From the pen of Rousseau comes a line that is short but filled with

16

truth: "Patience is bitter, but its fruit sweet." It will help us to have a happier life here, and will be an invaluable help in preparation for life eternal. We can make patience a habit if we will carefully consider what it is, and determine to practice it each day. The reward will be well worth our effort.

Fill in Scriptures

1. _____In your patience possess ye your souls.

2. _____And not only so, but we glory in tribulations also; knowing that tribulations worketh patience.

3. _____For ye have need of patience that, after ye have done the will of God, ye might receive the promise.

4. _____We ourselves glory in you in the churches of God for your patience and faith in all your persecutions and tribulations that ye endure.

5. _____Rejoicing in hope; patient in tribulation; continuing instant in prayer.

6. _____But if we hope for that we see not, then do we with patience wait for it.

7. _____But in all things approving ourselves as the ministers of God, in much patience, in afflictions, in necessities in distresses.

8. _____Be not slouthful, but followers of them who through faith and patience inherit the promise.

9. _____Knowing this that the trying of your faith worketh patience.

10. _____Ye have heard of the patience of Job.

11. _____I waited patiently for the Lord; and he inclined unto me, and heard my cry.

12. _____And so, after he had patiently endured, he obtained the promise.

Romans 5:3 KJV   Romans 8:25 KJV   James 1:3 KJV
Hebrews 10:36 KJV   Luke 21:19 KJV   Psalms 40:1 KJV
2 Thessalonians 1:4 KJV 2 Corinthians 6:4 KJV Hebrews 6:15 KJV
Romans 12:12 KJV   Hebrews 6:12 KJV   James 5:11 KJV

Questions for Discussion

1. Define patience.
2. Are you longsuffering toward the weakness, faults, intriacies, and unseemly manners of others?
3. Name several situations where it takes much patience.
4. Do you immediately become visibly shaken when others oppose you, or try to correct you , or falsely accuse you?
5. What does it mean to become "weary in well-doing"?
6. Are you easily discouraged?
7. Have you ever commended someone who patiently endured under prolonged trials or hostility?
8. What other excellent traits may develop in trials besides patience?
9. How is patience developed?
10. Summarize the need, blessings and rewards of patience.

Suggested Assignments

1. Memorize Romans 5:3, Romans 12:12.
2. Make sentences with the following: endurance, fortitude, submission, self-control; long suffering.
3. Visit a convalescent home.
4. Report on the first two chapters of Job.

Obedience

The great apostle Paul wrote, "Children, obey your parents in everything, for this pleases the Lord" (Colossians 3:20). And again, "Children, obey your parents in the Lord, for this is right. 'Honor your father and mother' (this is the first commandment with a promise), 'that it may be well with you and that you may live long on the earth'" (Ephesians 6:1-3).

Obedience is defined as the act or state of yielding willingly to the control or command of others; submission to authority or law; dutifulness.

The willingness to conform to the right and wishes of those in authority is a most desirable quality for any individual to possess. The jails and prisons of our land are filled with individuals who do not possess this quality. Those who learn early in life the importance of proper respect for law and order will usually throughout adult life cheerfully conform to the rules and regulations which society has established for the common good of all. Obedience in its broader sense means more than carrying out the request of the parent or the command of a superior officer; it means cheerfully and gladly executing promptly the task we are expected to perform.

The person who learns in early childhood to respect the rights of society and the wishes of other people will be most happy in the performance of those duties which are certainly going to fall to his or her lot during life. Those who prosper most and who enjoy life to the fullest degree will be in constant obedience to the rules, laws and regulations of society, nature, and above all, God. Those who disobey or break the rules and laws will be unhappy and will suffer hardships which might otherwise have been avoided.

We cannot hope to accomplish much in this life if we do not conform to and obey the rules of the society in which we live. The father of the great Carthaginian general, Hannibal, said, "My son Hannibal will be a great general because of all my soldiers he best knows how to obey."

If we learn to obey our parents, teachers, and the laws of our country, it will be easier for us to obey the Lord, and to become great soldiers in the battle against sin. There is nothing more important than this as we can read in 2 Thessalonians 1:7-9, ". . . when the Lord Jesus is revealed from heaven with his mighty angels in flaming fire, inflicting vengeance upon those who do not know God and upon those who do not obey the gospel of our Lord Jesus. They shall suffer the punishment of eternal destruction and exclusion from the presence of the Lord and from the glory of his might."

We read in Hebrews, regarding Jesus our Savior, "Although he was a Son, he learned obedience through what he suffered; and being made perfect he became the source of eternal salvation to all who obey him" (Hebrews 5:8,9). Even Christ the Son of God, was obedient; how careful we should be to make this wonderful trait a part of our life.

Fill in Scriptures

1. _____The people of Israel . . . perished, because they did not hearken to the voice of the Lord.

2. _____Because I have called and you refused to listen . . . and you have ignored all my counsel . . . I also will laugh at your calamity.

3. _____Remind them to be submissive to rulers and authorities, to be obedient, to be ready for any honest work.

4. _____This command I gave them, "Obey my voice, and I will be your God, and you shall be my people. . ."

5. _____Not everyone who says to me, 'Lord, Lord', shall enter the Kingdom of heaven, but he who does the will of my father who is in heaven.

6. _____And if you obey the voice of the Lord your God, being careful to do all his commandments which I command you this day, the Lord your God will set you high above all the nations of the earth.

7. _____But if you will not obey the voice of the Lord your God

or be careful to do all his commandments and his statutes which I command you this day, then all these curses shall come upon you and overtake you.

8._____Thy will be done on earth as it is in heaven.

9._____A man who has violated the law of Moses dies without mercy at the testimony of two or three witnesses. How much worse punishment do you think will be deserved by the man who has spurned the Son of God.

10._____Although he was a son, he learned obedience through what he suffered; and being made perfect he became the source of eternal salvation to all who obey him.

11._____Children, obey your parents in the Lord, for this is right. "Honor your father and mother" . . . "that it may be well with you and that you may live long on the earth."

Ephesians 6:1-3	Proverbs 1:24-26	Hebrews 5:8,9
Joshua 5:6	Jeremiah 7:23	Matthew 6:10
Titus 3:1	Matthew 7:21	Hebrews 10:28,29
Deuteronomy 28:15	Deuteronomy 28:1	

Questions for Discussion

1. Define obedience.
2. What do men hope to gain by breaking the law?
3. It has been estimated that there have been 33 million laws inacted since creation. In your estimation what is the greatest law?
4. Name some common ways that children sometimes disobey parents.
5. Name some common ways that men break the laws of the land.
6. Name some common ways that God's laws are broken.
7. What is God's attitude toward disobedience?
8. Are laws made to please everyone?
9. Why is it necessary that there be limits, boundaries and submissiveness in all realms whether it be in the natural, Spiritual, or social?
10. Who is qualified to make regulations, rules and laws?
11. How exacting are rules in sports?

12. What kind of catastrophe would strike us if suddenly the sun, moon and stars and the whole solar system would leave their determined track and cease to obey God's natural laws?

13. Suppose all nations of earth would disregard all fixed boundaries and the larger and more powerful countries would gobble up the smaller ones and the only lines left were ones where force could not cross over. What would be the end results.?

14. What would it be like if all citizens in the U.S.A. were to disregard all laws and each person did what was right in his own eye?

15. Since God created us, sustains us, and knows what is best for us—should he not have the right to govern us?

16. Summarize the need, blessings, and rewards of obedience.

Suggested Assignments

1. Memorize Matthew 7:21; Hebrews 5:9

2. Study and report on disobedience in the case of Korah, Numbers 16:1—35; and that of Nadab and Abihu found in Leviticus 10:1-7.

Reliability

Jesus said, "He who is faithful in a very little is faithful also in much; and he who is dishonest in very little is dishonest also in much. If then you have not been faithful in the unrighteous mammon, who will entrust to you the true riches? And if you have not been faithful in that which is another's, who will give you that which is your own?" (Luke 16:10-12).

Reliability is the state or quality of meriting trust or confidence; trustworthiness; dependability.

One of life's greatest achievements is reliability. It greatly increases man's opportunity for obtaining both wealth and power, and affords him the satisfaction of having the confidence of his friends and associates.

Reliability differs from responsibility in that it demonstrates by our past actions how much we can be depended upon to carry out our duties or responsibilities. In other words, reliability shows our trustworthiness regarding our obligations.

Gifford Pinchot, American politician and writer, said, "There is no more valuable subordinate than the man to whom you can give a piece of work and then forget it, in the confident expectation that the next time it is brought to your attention it will come in the form of a report that the thing has been done. When this self-reliant quality is joined to executive power, loyalty and common sense, the result is a man whom you can trust. On the other hand, there is no greater nuisance to a man heavily burdened with the direction of affairs than the weak-backed assistant who is continually trying to avoid his responsibility on the feeble plea that he thought the chief would like to decide this or that himself. The man to whom an executive is most grateful, the man whom he will work hardest and value most, is the man who accepts responsibility willingly.''

The apostle Paul, writing to the Corinthians, said, "this is how one should regard us, as servants of Christ and stewards of the mysteries of God. Moreover, it is required of stewards that they be found trustworthy" (1 Corinthians 4:1,2). God has no need of us in his kingdom if we cannot be relied upon to do his will anymore than men would tolerate us in the business world if we proved lacking in reliability.

We can make reliability one of our characteristic traits if we will always be certain to meet each of our responsibilities to the best of our ability. We must never enter into any agreements or make any promises which we cannot fulfill. Our obligations must be fulfilled, even if it be to our momentary disadvantage, because in time our gain will be great, in honor at least, which will make the momentary loss seem trivial.

Fill in Scriptures

1. _____ So that we may no longer be children tossed to and fro and carried about with every wind of doctrine.

2. _____ His trust is as a spider's web.

3. _____ Beware lest you be carried away with the error of lawless men and lose your own stability.

4. _____ He is like a tree planted by streams of water.

5. _____ The Lord hates . . . a lying tongue . . . a heart that devises wicked plans . . . a false witness who breathes out lies.

6. _____ Who then is the faithful and wise servant.

7. _____ He who endures to the end will be saved.

8. _____ These are . . . waterless clouds, carried along by winds; fruitless trees . . . wild waves of the sea . . . wandering stars for whom the nether gloom of darkness has been reserved for ever.

9. _____ Therefore, my beloved brethren, be steadfast, immovable, always abounding in the work of the Lord.

10. _____ Be faithful unto death and I will give you the crown of life.

11. _____ The heart of her husband trusts in her.

12._____He who trusts in his riches will wither.

13._____Suffering produces endurance, and endurance produces character.

14._____A man had two sons; and he went to the first and said, "Son, go and work in the vineyard today." and he answered, "I will not." but afterwards he repented and went. And he went to the second and said the same; and he answered, "I go, sir," but did not go. Which of the two did the will of his father?

15._____For that person must not suppose that a double-minded man, unstable in all his ways, will receive anything from the Lord.

James 1:7	Proverbs 6:16-19	Psalms 1:3
2 Peter 3:17	Job 8:14	Ephesians 4:14
Proverbs 11:28	Jude 12-13	Matthew 21:28-31
Romans 5:3-4	Proverbs 31:11	Matthew 10:22
Revelation 2:10	1 Corinthians 15:58	Matthew 24:45

Questions for Discussion

1. Define reliability.
2. Do you feel that this is one of your strong characteristics?
3. Is this a natural quality or one that must be developed?
4. Do you have doubts about others' reliability?
5. Do others question your dependability?
6. How does one prove his dependability?
7. Have you ever been adversely affected by another's lack of reliability?
8. Is it wise to trust everyone explicitly?
9. Should successive trials and discouragements affect one's reliability?
10. Can you be relied upon to carry out responsibilities assigned you without continual prodding, even in trying circumstances?
11. Have you broken promises or made statements that can't be supported?
12. Would you wish to marry, or be in business with one who is unreliable?

13. How important are strong determination, willpower, and friendship in establishing one's reliability?
14. Can you be relied upon to: be faithful in attendance to Bible class; be there on time; get lessons and make contributions to class studies?
15. Are you invariably making the same mistakes over and over?
16. Summarize the need, blessings and rewards of reliability.

Suggested Assignments

1. Memorize Ephesians 4:14; Proverbs 6:16-19.
2. Make sentences of the following words: dependable, trustworthy, veracity, genuine, reliable.
3. Take notes on the preacher's sermon.
4. Prayerfully consider ways by which you can enlist someone to come to your Bible class.

Respect

"We beseech you, brethren, to respect those who labor among you and are over you in the Lord and admonish you, and to esteem them very highly in love because of their work" (1 Thess. 5:12-13).

To respect is to honor duly; revere; esteem; treat with consideration; or to regard as of interest or importance; as, a wise man respects public opinion. It might also mean to avoid intruding upon; as, to respect private property.

This is a quality of mind that is shown by acts of deference and honor. It is easy to be respectful to one whom we regard as worth of esteem. And it is interesting to note the variety of people that are admired. Some men admire a famous ball player more than they do a famous inventor or scientist. Boys usually admire men who can perform feats of strength, while girls are more likely to respect the possessor of grace or beauty. Our admiration usually turns to what we can best understand, if it appeals to us at all. The reason some people admire cheap and unworthy things is that they cannot understand anything better. We must train ourselves so that our respect and admiration will be directed toward those who are truly worthy of esteem.

Having its beginning in the mind, respect cannot be forced from without, but we can cultivate within ourselves a cordial and loving spirit. By being thoughtfully considerate of our associates we can acquire the habit of performing the small acts which are marks of respect. Holding the door open for someone with a burden, allowing older people to enter or leave a room first, offering a chair to one who is standing, or any of the many other little acts of politeness and consideration, will do much to enrich our lives and the lives of those about us.

Respect is reciprocal in that if one wishes to gain respect from others he himself must show respect for them. The receiver must first be the giver. To have respect one must be respectable. We are taught in the scriptures to esteem those highly that are over us and to respect those who labor among us in the Lord. Only the thoughtless and the ignorant fail to show acts of deference and honor. "Let the greatest among you become as the youngest, and the leader as one who serves" (Luke 22:26 RSV). We must not look upon others with discrimination. Even the poor, the meek and the most humble are worthy of honor and respect. "He who is greatest among you shall be your servant" (Matthew 23:11 RSV).

"First of all, then, I urge that supplications, prayers, intercessions, and thanksgivings be made for all men, for kings and all who are in high positions, that we may lead a quiet and peaceable life, godly and respectful in everyway" (1 Timothy 2:1-2).

Fill in Scriptures

1. _____Out do one another in showing honor.

2. _____You shall rise up before the hoary head, and honor the face of an old man, and you shall fear your God; I am the Lord.

3. _____Honor widows who are real widows.

4. _____Honor your father and mother (this is the first commandment with a promise), "that it may be well with you and that you may live long on the earth."

5. _____Therefore, if food is a cause of my brother's falling, I will never eat meat, lest I cause my brother to fall.

6. _____But we beseech you, brethren, to respect those who labor among you and are over you in the Lord and admonish you, and esteem them very highly in love because of their work.

7. _____Do nothing from selfishness or conceit, but in humility count others better than yourself.

8. _____Honor all men. Love the brotherhood. Fear God. Honor the emperor.

9. _____Likewise you husbands, live considerately with your wives, bestowing honor on the woman as the weaker sex, since you are joint heirs of the grace of life in order that

your prayers may not be hindered.

10._____Let the elders who rule well be considered worthy of double honor, especially those who labor in preaching and teaching.

11._____On the contrary the parts of the body which seem to be weaker are indispensable, and those parts of the body which we think less honorable we invest with the greater honor and our unpresentable parts are treated with greater modesty.

12._____My brethren, show no partiality.

13._____Let every person be subject to the governing authorities.

1 Corinthians 8:13	Romans 12:10	1 Timothy 5:3
Leviticus 19:32	1 Timothy 5:17	James 2:1
1 Corinthians 12:22-23	1 Peter 3:7	1 Peter 2:17
Romans 13:1	1 Thessalonians 5:12-13	Philippians 2:3
Ephesians 6:2-3		

Questions for Discussion

1. Define respect.
2. Where is respect lacking the most?
3. Why do you suppose God commands that we pay particular attention to widows?
4. How does one show esteem to the elders?
5. Why are we commanded to have special regard for governing authorities?
6. What do you respect the most in a person?
7. How can one readily lose his respect?
8. Suggest several ways that children can manifest their honor and respect for parents.
9. Does the church where you attend have the respect of the community?
10. How did the early church gain the "favor of all the people"?
11. Summarize the need, blessings and rewards of showing proper respect.

Suggest Assignments

1. Memorize Ephesians 6:2,3; 1 Thessalonians 5:12,13.
2. Make up sentences using the following words: respect, esteem, honor, courtesy.
3. Express your appreciation to someone in church or school either in person or by writing a card.

Friendship

Jesus said, "This is my commandment, that you love one another as I have loved you. Greater love has no man than this, that a man lay down his life for his friends. You are my friends if you do what I command you" (John 15:12-14).

Friendship is defined as being a mutual attachment coupled with affection, regard or esteem.

Among the most beautiful of the examples of friendship given us in the Bible is the friendship of David and Jonathan, the son of King Saul. "And it came to pass, when he had made an end of speaking unto Saul, that the soul of Jonathan was knit with the soul of David, and Jonathan loved him as his own soul" (1 Samuel 18:1 KJV).

Solomon, the man of wisdom, said, "A man that hath friends must shew himself friendly: and there is a friend that sticketh closer than a brother" (Proverbs 18:24 KJV). To have friends we must be a friend; we cannot expect anyone else to care for us if we don't regard them with affection anymore than we care for those who have no regard for us. The Bible tells us that even our love for God exists because He first loved us. In 1 John 4:19 we read, "We love, because he first loved us."

It is God's will that we have friendship with one another. He loves us, and wants us to love our brothers and sisters in Christ. This is the way we show our love for Him: by being obedient to His commandments and loving His children. "If any one says, 'I love God,' and hates his brother, he is a liar; for he who does not love his brother whom he has seen, cannot love God whom he has not seen. And this commandment we have from him, that he who loves God should love his brother also" (1 John 4:20,21).

32

In Proverbs 27:9 we read, "Ointment and perfume rejoice the heart: so doth the sweetness of a man's friend by hearty counsel" (KJV). Those who are friends do not look after their own interests at the expense of one another, but will help and encourage each other in mutual love and understanding.

We must take care that the friendships we form are with those who are worthy of being called "friend." We may have many acquaintances who are not friends in the fullest sense of the word. James said, "Unfaithful creatures! Do you not know that friendship with the world is enmity with God? Therefore whoever wishes to be a friend of the world makes himself an enemy of God" (James 4:4). By "the world" James means those persons who do not love God, but are interested merely in the material things of this life. We are to try to teach them God's word and to create a love for God in them, but they are not to be our friends as God would have us be friends with our fellow Christians. We can always treat them kindly, and do what we can to help them, but must not share their worldly pleasures lest we be lead away from God.

We must be careful, then, in the friendships we form and we must treasure our friendships and nourish them with loving thoughtfulness and kindness.

Fill in Scriptures

1. _____Julius treated Paul kindly, and gave him leave to go to his friends and be cared for.

2. _____A man that hath friends must shew himself friendly: and there is a friend that sticketh closer than a brother.

3. _____And the natives showed us unusual kindness, for they kindled a fire and welcomed us all, because it had begun to rain and was cold.

4. _____Now when Job's three friends heard of all this evil that had come upon him, they came each from his own place . . . to . . . comfort him.

5. _____Go home to your friends, and tell them how much the Lord has done for you.

6. _____A whisperer separates close friends.

7. _____Let your foot be seldom in your neighbor's house lest he become weary of you and hate you.

8._____Faithful are the wounds of a friend; profuse are the kisses of an enemy.

9._____Make no friendship with a man given to anger.

10._____He who witholds kindness from a friend forsakes the fear of the Almighty.

11._____Everyone is a friend to a man who gives gifts.

12._____A friend loves at all times.

Proverbs 18:24 KJV Acts 27:3 Proverbs 16:28
Job 2:11 Mark 5:19 Proverbs 27:6
Proverbs 25:17 Proverbs 22:24 Proverbs 17:17
Job 6:14 Acts 28:2 Proverbs 19:6

Questions for Discussion
1. Define friendship.
2. How does one make friends?
3. How does one keep friends?
4. Who might be a "fair weather friend"?
5. What is the greatest thing one might do for his friend?
6. What kind of friends should one seek?
7. Is it always wrong to be friends with sinners?
8. Why does James condemn "friendship with the world"?
9. How can friendship be spoiled?
10. What should one do who has a habit of losing his friends?
11. Have you ever had a friend that tried to smother you and possess your time?
12. Summarize the need, blessings and rewards of friendship.

Suggested Assignments:
1. Show yourself friendly this week to a person that you presently do not know.
2. Visit in the home of one who is a new member or someone who visited in your assembly at church.
3. Invite someone to Bible Class.
4. Memorize: John 15:12-14.

5. Make sentences with the following words: snobbish, clannish, friendly.

Generosity

"If any one has the world's goods and sees his brother in need, yet closes his heart against him, how does God's love abide in him? Little children, let us not love in word or speech but in deed and in truth" (1 John 3:17,18).

Generosity is defined as the quality of being liberal; breadth of opinion; of a free and bountiful spirit.

Usually, the word "generosity" is associated with the thought of money, and one is considered to be generous when he is liberal with his financial resources. In a larger sense, however, it means liberality of spirit or "large-mindedness." A person's generosity with money might grow out of failure to realize its worth or from the fact that the money is earned and hence not fully appreciated as to its value, but one who is truly generous displays that characteristic because he feels liberal in spirit. The actual money involved is but a means of expression for the desire to be helpful and to take others into one's heart. A truly generous person is also kind and considerate.

There are many examples of generosity on the part of individuals recorded in the Bible. In Acts 2:45 we read: "and they sold their possessions and goods and distributed them to all, as any had need." And in Acts 4:34,35: "There was not a needy person among them, for as many as were possessors of lands or houses sold them, and brought the proceeds of what was sold and laid it at the apostles' feet; and distribution was made to each as any had need."

The apostle Paul, writing to the Corinthians, said, "We want you to know, brethren, about the grace of God which has been shown in the churches of Macedonia, for in a severe test of affliction, their abundance of joy and their extreme poverty have overflowed in a wealth of liberality on their part. For they gave according to their means, as I can testify, and beyond their means, of their own free will, begging us earnestly for the favor of taking part in the relief of the saints—and this, not as we expected, but first they gave themselves to the Lord and to us by the will of God'' (2 Corinthians 8:1-5).

To the Philippians Paul wrote, "Yet it was kind of you to share my trouble. And you Philippians yourselves know that in the beginning of the gospel, when I left Macedonia, no church entered into partnership with me in giving and receiving except you only; for even in Thessalonica you sent me help once and again. Not that I seek the gift; but I seek the fruit which increases to your credit. I have received full payment, and more; I am filled, having received from Epaphroditus the gifts you sent, a fragrant offering, a sacrifice acceptable and pleasing to God'' (Phil. 4:14-18).

Liberality of spirit is truly pleasing and acceptable to God. Those early Christians abounded in love and generosity; they didn't give of their surplus, but in their poverty shared their very sustenance.

How can we develop generosity? First, we can give more thoughtful consideration to other people and their needs. Then when we see a need, we can give to them out of that which we have. It is not a spirit of generosity on our part to pass along something which someone else has. When we give money for the Lord's work, it is money that we have earned? If we are merely "handing over" money that has been given us for that purpose we are not training ourselves in generosity.

A wise mother in training her little son to be generous used the opportunity of his desire to feed the hungry birds that flitted in the snow outside the window. Instead of handing him a piece of bread and saying, "Break this up and feed the birds," she waited until time for the meal and then suggested that he take part of his own piece of bread and give it to the hungry birds outside. She realized that only when one gives that which is his own, is he really giving.

Fill in Scriptures

1. _____And Zacchaeus stood and said to the Lord, "Behold, Lord the half of my goods I give to the poor."

2. _____If any one has the world's goods and sees his brother in need, yet closes his heart against him, how does God's love abide in him?

3. _____I say unto you, Love your enemies and pray for those

who persecute you, so that you may be sons of your Father who is in heaven; for he makes his sun rise on the evil and on the good.

4._____On the first day of every week, each of you is to put something aside and store it up, as he may prosper.

5._____If your enemy is hungry, feed him.

6._____Will a man rob God? Yet you are robbing me. But you say, "How are we robbing thee?" In your tithes and offerings.

7._____The people bring much more than enough for doing the work . . . So Moses gave command . . . "Let neither man nor woman do anything more for the offering for the sanctuary." So the people were restrained from bringing.

8._____God so loved the world that he gave his only Son.

9._____In all things I have shown you that by so toiling one must help the weak, remembering the words of the Lord Jesus, how he said, "It is more blessed to give than to receive."

10._____Our heart is wide. You are not restricted by us, but you are restricted in your own affections. In return—I speak as to children— widen your hearts also.

11._____He who sows sparingly will also reap sparingly . . . God loves a cheerful giver.

12._____I will not offer . . . to the Lord my God which cost me nothing.

1 John 3:17	Romans 12:20	Exodus 36:5-6
Matthew 5:44-45	Acts 20:35	2 Corinthians 9:6-7
Luke 19:8	Malachi 3:8	2 Samuel 24:24
1 Corinthians 16:2	John 3:16	2 Corinthians 6:11-13

Questions for Discussion

1. Define generosity.
2. What should be the true motive for giving, sharing and doing for others?
3. What is God's attitude toward the liberal giver?

4. What does it mean not to give "grudgingly" or "reluctantly"?

5. Name several ways one may exercise his generosity.

6. Let's assume that we have 2,500,000 church members in America. If we could efficiently challenge only one fifth of that number, that is, 500,000 to sacrifice 15¢ a day for the Lord's work above their regular contribution for a year, what would the sum total be?

7. How may we motivate others to greater generosity?

8. We read in Colossians 3:5, "covetousness, which is idolatry," and in 1 Corinthians 10:19, 20 we find that idolatry is associated with demons. Where, then, does this place the person who hold back his liberality from the Lord.

9. Which is the most difficult to accomplish—being a good giver or a good receiver?

10. Name ten of your greatest blessings received from God.

11. Name ten of the greatest blessings received from others.

12. Summarize the need, blessings and rewards of generosity.

Suggested Assignments

1. Miss a meal this week and contribute the money to the Lord.

2. Send a sympathy card to a family where there has been a death. You may use the obituary column of the newspaper.

3. Make a report on the yearly contribution of the church where you attend. Report how much was spent on benevolence, on edification, and on evangelism.

4. Make sentences of the following words: liberal, stingy, sacrifice, covetousness.

Happiness

"The faith that you have, keep between yourself and God; happy is he who has no reason to judge himself for what he approves" (Romans 14:22).

Happiness is the state or quality of being glad or pleased; joyfulness; delight; radiant pleasure.

The constitution upon which our great country is based speaks of the right of all men to life, liberty and the pursuit of happiness. Most every one will agree that happiness is important, for without it whatever else we may gain of a material nature seems of little value to us. What do dollars, or station in life, or position mean if there is no happiness? On the other hand, a person might be happy even though poor. Happiness is not found in circumstances of wealth, nor in the lack of it. If one has acquired characteristic cheerfulness it is much more likely that he will find true happiness. In our search for happiness we must first realize that it cannot be secured by wrong or evil means. It is in service to others, in deeds of kindness and mercy, in generosity and forgiveness, that we can find the greatest pleasure possible. Jesus taught this to his disciples after the last supper when he washed their hot, tired and dusty feet, which was a service they could fully appreciate. Then he told them that he had given them an example so that they would be of service to others, and said, "if you know these things, blessed are you if you do them" (John 13:17).

The English writer George Eliot expressed this great truth regarding happiness, "It is only a poor sort of happiness that could ever come by caring very much about our own narrow pleasures. We can only have the highest happiness, such as goes along with being a great man, by having wide thoughts, and much feeling for the rest of the world as well as ourselves; and this sort of happiness often brings

40

so much pain with it, that we can only tell it from pain by its being what we would choose before everything else, because our souls see it is good."

Christians should be the happiest people in the world for they have God's Word to guide them in this life, and the promise of salvation in the life beyond if they will obey him. James admonished Christians to "Be patient, therefore, brethren, until the coming of the Lord . . . Behold, we call those happy who were steadfast" (James 5:7,11).

It has been said, "The secret of happiness is not in doing what one likes, but in liking what one has to do." By serving the Lord, and each other, we will have true happiness.

Fill in Scriptures

1._____These things I have spoken to you, that my joy may be in you, and that your joy may be full.

2._____And all who believed were together and had all things in common; and they sold their possessions and goods and distributed them to all, as any had need. And day by day, attending the temple together and breaking bread in their homes, they partook of food with glad and generous hearts.

3._____The fruit of the Spirit is love, joy, peace.

4._____I rejoiced greatly to find some of your children following the truth, just as we have been commanded by the Father.

5._____Happy is the man who finds wisdom, and the man who gets understanding for the gain from it is better than gain from silver and its profit better than gold.

6._____Happy is he whose help is the God of Jacob, whose hope is in the Lord his God, who made heaven and earth, the sea, and all that is in them; who keeps faith forever; who executes justice for the oppressed; who gives food to the hungry.

7._____Happy is he who is kind to the poor.

8._____He who finds his life will lose it, and he who loses his life for my sake will find it.

9._____Then they left the presence of the council, rejoicing that they were counted worthy to suffer dishonor for the name.

10._____Blessed is every one who fears the Lord, who walks in his ways! You shall eat the fruit of the labor of your hands; you shall be happy, and it shall be well with you.

Psalms 128:1-2   Galatians 5:22   Acts 5:41
2 John 4   Psalms 146:5-7   Acts 2:44-46
Matthew 10:39   Proverbs 3:13-14   Proverbs 14:21
John 15:11

Questions for Discussion

1. Define happiness. ✓
2. Is happiness an universal desire?
3. Can we find happiness by seeking it directly, or is it a by-product?
4. Does everyone have the right to be happy?
5. Jesus found happiness and fulfillment in primarily four ways:
   (A) In a book (the Bible).
   (B) Rendering a deep, abiding service for God and mankind.
   (C) Social life (He loved people and enjoyed friendship).
   (D) He loved nature (God's picture book), the outdoors.
   Are you seeking inward peace and happiness the same way?
6. The early Christians were flogged for their faith; still they rejoiced for being counted worthy to suffer for Christ's cause. ~~Can you explain this?~~ Why
7. How does a person keep himself from boredom?
8. Does every person have in his power the ability to make others happy?
9. Explain what Jesus meant when he spoke of joy that no one could take away from you.
10. Can circumstances or things that happen to us permanently destroy inward peace and joy that comes from knowing Christ?
11. Is it possible for an unhappy Christian to influence others for Christ?
12. Why are many people unhappy even though they possess much wealth, popularity, beauty, and exalted position?
13. Summarize the need of happiness.

Suggested Assignment

1. Memorize Acts 2:44-46.

2. Make sentences of the following words: joy, cheerful, gloomy, bleak.

3. Try to cheer or lift the spirit of someone this week.

Morality

We read in Titus 2:12, ". . . denying ungodliness and worldly lusts, we should live soberly, righteously and godly, in this present world" (KJV).

Morality is righteousness; virtue; the teaching or practice of the duties of life; discrimination between right and wrong.

There are accepted standards of what is right, and morality is conformity with those standards. A Christian must obey God's standards as revealed to us in the New Testament, and also the customs and laws of the society in which he lives, so long as they do not conflict with God's laws.

A person is immoral when he knowingly violates the standards of God, and is regarded as moral when he observes them and is a good example of them. God's laws are to ALL people for all time. When we obey His laws we will be morally acceptable anywhere.

We read in His Word, "Be subject for the Lord's sake to every human institution, whether it be to the emperor as supreme, or to govenors as sent by him to punish those who do wrong and to praise those who do right. For it is God's will that by doing right you should put to silence the ignorance of foolish men. Live as freemen, yet without using your freedom as a pretext for evil; but live as servants of God. Honor all men. Love the brotherhood. Fear God. Honor the emperor " (1 Peter 2:13-17).

Each of us must strive daily to make morality a part of our character so that we will be righteous before God. Solomon wrote in Psalms 37:39, "The salvation of the righteous is from the Lord; He is their refuge in the time of trouble."

A casual glance at our society should convince all that we are in a moral crisis. There are many who now suggest that we cannot be certain what is actually right or wrong. The permissive philosophy has done much to destroy the decent standards of God. Isaiah declared "Woe to them that call evil good and good evil, that put darkness for light and light for darkness" (Isaiah 5:20 RSV). Moses announced, "Thou shalt not follow a multitude to do evil" (Ex 23:2 RSV). And the Apostle Paul said, "He that soweth to the flesh shall of the flesh reap corruption" (Galatians 6:8 RSV).

Before nations fall they become immoral and obsessed with all manner of sexual abuses. They lose their sense of decency, and disregard law and order. Morality then is necessary for our survival. What the earth needs is cleansed, empowered personalities. No marvel that the Bible states clearly that without holiness no man shall see God (Hebrews 12:14). We must be able to discriminate between right and wrong, fight for decency and oppose all that which tends to moral decay.

Fill in Scriptures

1. _____Let no one despise your youth, but set the believers an example in speech and conduct, in love, in faith, in purity.

2. _____I say to you that every one who divorces his wife, except on the ground of unchastity, makes her an adulteress; and whoever marries a divorced woman commits adultry.

3. _____But immorality and all impurity or covetousness must not even be named among you, as is fitting among saints. Let there be no filthiness, nor silly talk, nor levity, which are not fitting; but instead let there be thanksgiving. Be sure of this, that no immoral or impure man, or one who is covetous (that is, an idolater), has any inheritance in the kingdom of Christ.

4. _____Religion that is pure and undefiled before God and the Father is this: to visit orphans and widows in their affliction, and to keep oneself unstained in the world.

5. _____Let marriage be held in honor among all, and let the marriage bed be undefiled; for God will judge the immoral and adulterous.

6. _____Shun youthful passions and aim at righteousness . . . call upon the Lord from a pure heart.

7._____Now the works of the flesh are plain: immorality, impurity, licenteousness, idolatry, sorcery, enmity, strife . . . that those who do such things shall not inherit the kingdom of God.

8._____The lips of a loose woman drip honey, and her speech is smoother than oil; but in the end she is bitter as wormwood, sharp as a two-edged sword. Her feet go down to death.

9._____We must not indulge in immorality as some of them did, and twenty-three thousand fell in a single day.

Ephesians 5:3-5   Matthew 5:32   1 Timothy 4:12
1 Corinthians 10:8   Proverbs 5:3-5   Galatians 5:19-21
2 Timothy 2:22   Hebrews 13:4   James 1:27

Questions for Discussion

1. Define good morals.
2. How good are the generally accepted moral standards of our society?
3. "How can the young secure their hearts and guard their lives from sin?"
4. Do evil companions corrupt good moral standards?
5. How can we help one another to maintain good moral standards?
6. What affect do X-rated movies, pornographic literature, suggestive songs, loose talk have on our society?
7. What part do the following play in encouraging immorality: popularity, selfishness, money, ignorance, lustful curiosity?
8. What does this Scripture mean, "Righteousness exalts a nation"?
9. Where and when might be the time and place most susceptible to wrong standards?
10. What effect does morals have on the conscience, marriage, self-respect, health, happiness, and eternity?
11. Summarize the need, blessing and rewards of good morals.

Statement:"Sex is good. God thought it up." However, it is not designed for public display. Even in private it can be just as evil, unless with the right person at the right place and time. Manhood is to be fulfilled in marriage only. There is a time and place for everything. Like the flag of our country, there is a place for it. It is not to be dragged into the dirt. Fertilizer is good and no doubt indirectly saves and sustains millions of lives. Yet, it would be ghastly on our dining table. To be confused of time and place of precious things is indeed a tragedy. A fire is a tremendous blessing but not in the attic of our house. "He who commits adultery has no sense" (Proverbs 6:32).

Both the Bible and history attest that before nations fall they decay morally. "Excessive freedom leads to slavery."

Suggested Assignments

1. Memorize Matthew 5:32; 2 Timothy 2:22.
2. Read Proverbs 5 and 6.
3. Make sentences of the following words: purity, morality, adultery, moral standards.

Ambition

"A slack hand causes poverty, but the hand of the diligent makes rich" (Proverbs 10:4). God has always condemned idleness, or slothfulness, in His children. Paul wrote to the Thessalonians, "For we hear that some of you are living in idleness, mere busybodies, not doing any work. Now such persons we command and exhort in the Lord Jesus Christ to do their work in quietness and to earn their own living. Brethren, do not be weary in well-doing" (2 Thessalonians 3:11-13). We must have ambition in order to do a good work. Ambition is the desire a person may have to achieve a certain goal, or to obtain some object. When properly used it brings about much good, both for the individual and others. It is the vital quality which drives a person on to success.

Without ambition we would become idle and slothful, and would fall into the same condemnation as some of the Thessalonians.

We should work diligently to arouse within ourselves the ambition to achieve great things, for where there is no ambition—no ideals for which to work or goals to attain—there is no action. Nothing will be accomplished and our lives will be useless. We will become drones, and be a burden to society and to those who love us, rather than useful and honorable citizens.

Ambition is necessary to success, but if it is a selfish ambition it will often work to the harm of the person, as well as to the detriment of others affected by it. If we study the lives of men and women who have achieved great and good things, it will encourage us to, thoughtfully and prayerfully, create within ourselves the ambition to do our best at all times.

No one admires the slouthful, lazy, indolent person. He is a living disgrace to all—even his own family. "If anyone will not work, let him not eat. For we hear that some of you are living in idleness, mere busybodies, not doing any work" (2 Thessalonians 3:10-11). Putting it in plain hard language, the person that refuses to work should starve to death—for the Bible declares "let him not eat." This is actually an imperative—a command. The habitually lazy person will not keep a job nor will he keep his friends.

Nehemiah speaks admirably of the people in his day. They were ambitious and hard-working in face of great opposition from the enemy. "For the people had a mind to work" (Nehemiah 4:6).

"Go to the ant, O sluggard; consider her ways, and be wise. Without having any chief, officer or ruler, she prepares her food in summer, and gathers her sustenance in harvest. How long will you lie there, O sluggard? When will you arise from your sleep? A little sleep, a little slumber, a little folding of the hands to rest, and poverty will come upon you like a vagabond" (Proverbs 6:6-11).

Fill in Scriptures

1. _____ He who is slack in his work is a brother to him who destroys.

2. _____ So that you may not be sluggish, but imitators of those who through faith and patience inherit the promises.

3. _____ Conduct yourselves wisely toward outsiders, making the most of the time.

4. _____ Through sloth the roof sinks in, and through indolence the house leaks.

5. _____ If any one will not work, let him not eat. For we hear that some of you are living in idleness, mere busybodies, not doing any work.

6. _____ Behold, this was the guilt of . . . Sodom: she and her daughters had pride, surfeit of food, and prosperous ease.

7. _____ I passed by the field of a sluggard, by the vineyard of a man without sense; and lo, it was all overgrown with thorns; the ground was covered with nettles, and its stone wall was broken down.

8. _____ For you remember our labor and toil, brethren; we worked night and day, that we might not burden any of you, while we preached to you the gospel.

9._____ All night he continued in prayer.

10._____ My Father is working still and I am working.

11._____ My beloved brethren, be steadfast, immovable, always abounding in the work of the Lord, knowing that in the Lord your labor is not in vain.

12._____ She looks well to the ways of her household, and does not eat the bread of idleness. Her children rise up and call her blessed.

13._____ You wicked and slothful servant!

14._____ And every work that he undertook . . . he did with all his heart, and prospered.

1 Thessalonians 2:9	John 5:17	1 Corinthians 15:58
2 Chronicles 31:21	Proverbs 31:27-28	Matthew 25:26
Ecclesiastes 10:18	2 Thessalonians 3:10-11	Ezekiel 16:49
Proverbs 24:30-31	Luke 6:12	Proverbs 18:9
Hebrews 6:12	Colossians 4:5	

Questions for Discussion

1. Define ambition.
2. Why do some have an inordinate desire for ease and comfort?
3. Is it always wrong to seek recognition, rank and high position?
4. Can one easily develop a selfish evil ambition?
5. How can the non-involved, lazy person affect the church?
6. What is God's attitude toward the indolent, slothful servant?
7. Is ambition a natural quality or one that is developed?
8. Name some short and long-range goals that all should be striving diligently for.
9. Have you ever volunteered for some unpleasant task at home or church activity?
10. Suggest how rebuke, reward and self-discipline can affect one's eagerness to serve.
11. List ways valuable time can be wasted.
12. Is it true that we often tend to imitate each other's actions and examples?
13. How can we help each other to be more ambitious?

14. Summarize the need, blessing and rewards of ambition.

Suggested Assignments
1. Memorize Hebrews 6:12; Proverbs 18:9.
2. Make sentences of the following words: indolent, ambitious, work, busy, idleness, lazy.
3. Arise 15 minutes earlier than usual each day this week to study the Scriptures and prepare for Bible class.

Adaptability

Paul wrote the Philippians, "Not that I complain of want; for I have learned, in whatever state I am, to be content" (Philippians 4:11).

Adaptability is the power, or ability, to adjust one's self to circumstances, to make things suitable, or to alter something in order to make it fit for a new use.

No one can live in this complex world of ours without being faced with many changes and the need for altering plans, however well laid those plans may be. Adaptability, then, is a highly desirable characteristic, and one well worth our every effort to cultivate. The person who can easily and quickly adjust to unexpected situations is equipped with one of the most important powers possessed by human beings. It is good to have plans and know what is to be done, and how and when, but it is, perhaps, even more important to be able to make necessary changes on short notice that will accomplish the desired result.

Adaptability also means our ability to accept other people and to consider their feelings. We may have unconsciously adjusted our lives to fit in with the lives of our family and friends, but are we able to manage ourselves upon occasion as to be acceptable to other people?

Paul said, "I have become all things to all men, that I might by all means save some" (1 Corinthians 9:22).

Everything Paul became was something he **was**, in truth, but would probably not have stressed had it not shown a kindred characteristic, or state of affairs, with those whom he would teach. In like manner, we might stress the points of harmony we have with those whom we meet, rather than our differences. This would not only give us more influence with them, and opportunity to show an example of Christian living, but would make life more pleasant.

Whenever circumstances make it necessary for us to change our plans, let us do so gracefully. Instead of harboring disappointment, let us adapt ourselves to the change and make something good of it. By continually striving to make the best out of those unexpected situations, we will be building "adaptability" into our character. This will do much toward assuring us of success in life.

Fill in Scriptures

1. _____ Not that I complain of want, for I have learned, in whatever state I am, to be content. I know how to be abased and I know how to abound; in any and all circumstances I have learned the secret of facing plenty and hunger, abundance and want. I can do all things in him who strengthens me.

2. _____ Beloved, do not be surprised at the fiery ordeal which comes upon you to prove you, as though something strange were happening to you.

3. _____ We know that in everything God works for good with those who love him.

4. _____ One thing I do, forgetting what lies behind and straining forward to what lies ahead.

5. _____ No temptation has overtaken you that is common to man. God is faithful, and he will not let you be tempted beyond your strength, but with the temptation will also provide the way of escape, that you may be able to endure it.

6. _____ In all thy ways acknowledge him, and he shall direct thy paths.

7. _____ Be content with what you have; for he has said, "I will never fail you nor forsake you." Hence we can confidently say, "The Lord is my helper, I will not be afraid."

8. _____ No, in all these things we are more than conquerors through him who loved us. For I am sure that neither death, nor life, nor angels, nor principalities, nor things present, nor things to come, nor powers, nor

height, nor depth, nor anything else in all creation, will be able to separate us from the love of God in Christ Jesus our Lord.

9. _____ For though I am free from all men, I have made myself a slave to all, that I might win the more. To the Jew I became a Jew, in order to win Jews; to those under the law I became as one under the law—that I might win those under the law. To those outside the law I became as one outside the law . . . that I might win those outside the law. To the weak I became weak, that I might win the weak. I have become all things to all men, that I might be all means save some. I do it all for the sake of the gospel, that I may share in its blessings.

10. _____ Even though I walk through the valley of the shadow of death I fear no evil.

1 Corinthians 9:19-23   Hebrews 13:5-6   Romans 8:37-39
Philippians 3:13   1 Peter 4:12   1 Corinthians 10:13
Romans 8:28   Proverbs 3:6 KJV   Philippians 4:11-13
Psalms 23:4

Questions for Discussion

1. Define adaptability.
2. Is change a constant thing in our society? If so, in what way?
3. How can true Christians be a strength and blessing to one another in times of adjustment and change?
4. What might be the problem with the person who is never able to "fit in" or adapt to a new situation?
5. How can the church render a special service to a transient community?
6. How can the person who is predominately concerned with his own interests be a hinderance to adaptability?
7. What is an introvert?
8. What is an extravert?
9. Why couldn't the children of Israel adjust to the 40 years of wilderness wandering?
10. Joseph was put to almost every conceivable test: gross injury

to his brothers, favoritism of his father, solicitations of an impure woman, prison, sudden elevation to power and opportunity to avenge those who so severely injured him. Yet he gracefully came out on top and was a great example of adaptability. From this, suggest the one quality that, perhaps more than any other, enabled him to adjust.

11. Do you feel that most of us take our own problems too seriously and with too little faith?

12. Summarize the need, blessings, and rewards of adaptability.

Suggested Assignments

1. Memorize Romans 8:28; Proverbs 3:6.

2. Go all week without eating sweets or watching television.

3. Make an acquaintance with a new student in school, church, or in your community.

4. Go out of your way to help someone who has a need or problem.

Kindness

"Love one another with brotherly affection; outdo one another in showing honor" (Romans 12:10).

Kindness is the state or quality of being ready to do good to others; helpfulness, gentleness or graciousness.

It is a virtue based upon the ideal of consideration for others, or practicing what is generally called "the golden rule" of doing unto others as you would have them do unto you. It involves a wholesome attitude toward our associates and a willingness to help them. Kindness is the direct opposite of selfishness and cruelty, and is characterized by words or deeds which exhibit a spirit of helpfulness. Kindness softens the rough spots in our own lives, filling the dark days with joy and sunshine. Kind people are, as a rule, cheerful because when they help others over the difficult places in the road of life it not only gives joy to the ones who receive the service, but also brings happiness to themselves. All of us are striving for happiness, and when we recognize that acts of kindness to others always react to our own pleasure, we will do our best to cultivate this wonderful habit.

Let us heed the warning of the apostle Paul to the Ephesians, "Be kind to one another, tenderhearted, forgiving one another, as God in Christ forgave you" (Ephesians 4:32).

There are few characteristcs more important than kindness. It is easily detected and is powerful in its use. Kindness carries a tremendous impact on the lives of men, even animals. It is contageous, but often difficult to show to others when they fail to give it. "You made my day," people say to the one manifesting some act of kindness. It cheers the heart and brightens the day and causes the one who receives it to want to return it.

When you add the letter "d" to kin you have the word "kind." This is where the word comes from. "Kindness is the action of one kin to another." We are all in a sense, kin to Adam, and especially are we kin in Christ. We are brothers and sisters. Kindness is tied to kinship. God is kind to us for we are his kin—His children.

Police officers are often reluctant to answer calls to family fights. For they have learned that members of the family who have been quarreling and fighting against one another will often suddenly turn to unite in full force of their anger against the officer. When outside forces threaten, even families that fight with each other will stick together, because they are kin.

One of the most touching scenes of kindness is shown in the story of Abraham and Lot: "Abraham said to Lot, let there be no strife between you and me, and between your herdsmen and my herdsmen; for we are kindsmen."

Fill in Scriptures

1._____ Be kind to one another, tenderhearted, forgiving one another, as God in Christ forgave you.

2._____ Add to your faith . . . brotherly kindness; and to brotherly kindness charity.

3._____ And the natives showed us unusual kindness, for they kindled a fire and welcomed us all, because it had begun to rain and was cold.

4._____ But love your enemies, and do good, and lend, expecting nothing in return; and your reward will be great, and you will be sons of the Most High; for he is kind to the ungrateful and the selfish.

5._____ She opens her mouth with wisdom, and the teaching of kindness is on her tongue.

6._____ You have heard that it was said, "An eye for an eye and a tooth for a tooth." But I say to you, Do not resist one who is evil. But if any one strikes you on the right cheek, turn to him the other also.

7._____ Pray for those who persecute you.

8._____ I was hungry and you gave me food, I was thirsty and you gave me drink, I was a stranger and you welcomed me, I was naked and you clothed me, I was sick and you visited me.

9._____Love is patient and kind.

10._____If your enemy is hungry, feed him, if he is thirsty, give him drink.

11._____Love does not insist on its own way; it is not irritable or resentful.

12._____We who are strong ought to bear with the failings of the weak, and not to please ourselves.

Matthew 25:35-36   Matthew 5:44   Matthew 5:38-39
Proverbs 31:26   1 Corinthians 13:5   Romans 12:20
1 Corinthians 13:4   Luke 6:35   Acts 28:2
2 Peter 1:5-7 KJV   Ephesians 4:32   Romans 15:1

Questions for Discussion

1. Define kindness.
2. How important are gracious manners in the home?
3. Why aren't there more favors and kind deeds done, and more men and women with generous natures in our society?
4. What makes a person harsh, cruel and unfriendly?
5. How does one learn kindness?
6. When are we most likely to be lacking in forbearance, kindness, and warm feelings of goodwill?
7. What is the greatest kindness ever shown to you by another person?
8. What do you feel is the greatest kindness that you have shown to another?

Suggested Assignment

1. Memorize Ephesians 4:32; Luke 6:35.
2. Make sentences of the following words: kindness, forbearance, gracious, sympathy, kindly deeds, gentle, care.
3. Visit a shut-in, some aged one or a convalescent home.
4. Send a sympathy card to a family where there has been a death. Use the obituary column of the newspaper if necessary.

Cheerfulness

"A glad heart makes a cheerful countenance, but by sorrow of heart the spirit is broken" (Proverbs 15:13).

Cheerfulness is a state of gladness or joy; contentment; pleasantness; being of good spirit.

It is the quality of character that enables us to have the mental and spiritual attitude towards life which recognizes its events and views them in the most favorable, agreeable, and wholesome way possible. It is the ability to emphasize the good and minimize the unpleasant and unfavorable.

Everyone will have trials, but this will not hinder us from developing a spirit of cheerfulness and optimism if we can only realize their value to us. We read in Romans 8:28, "And we know that all things work together for good to them that love God, to them who are the called according to his purpose" (KJV). This assurance from God's Word should certainly help us to be of good cheer whenever we are faced with trouble, remembering that "the Lord disciplines him whom he loves, and chastises every son whom he receives," and that "for the moment all discipline seems painful rather than pleasant; later it yields the peaceful fruit of righteousness to those who have been trained by it" (Hebrews 12:6, 11).

Cheerfulness has been called "the oil of life that helps us to glide smoothly down the highway of time." It sustains us in time of trouble, and helps us over the rough places in our path.

It should be of encouragement to us to know that cheerfulness is a characteristic which can be acquired by each of us. As we begin to train ourselves in acquiring this worthwhile attitude we will have to use conscious effort, but repeated practice will make cheerfulness a habit, giving us a sense of pleasantness and an optimistic outlook toward life. Oliver Wendell Holmes said, "To be seventy years young is sometimes far more cheerful and hopeful than to be forty years old." In these words he is illustrating the importance of our attitude toward life.

Certainly all of us would like our journey through this world to be as pleasant as possible, so let us begin now to cultivate a spirit of cheerfulness.

Fill in Scriptures

1._____A cheerful heart is a good medicine, but a downcast spirit dries up the bones.

2._____But rejoice in so far as you share Christ's sufferings, that you may also rejoice and be glad when his glory is revealed.

3._____Take heart, my son; your sins are forgiven.

4._____Pleasant words are like a honeycomb, sweetness to the soul and health to the body.

5._____He that goes forth weeping, bearing the seed for sowing, shall come home with shouts of joy, bringing his sheaves with him.

6._____A glad heart makes a cheerful countenance but by sorrow of heart the spirit is broken.

7._____This is the day which the Lord had made; let us rejoice and be glad in it.

8._____I was glad when they said to me, "Let us go to the house of the Lord!"

9._____He did good and gave you from heaven rains and fruitful seasons, satisfying your hearts with food and gladness.

10._____Shout for joy and be glad, and say evermore, "Great is the Lord, who delights in the welfare of his servant!

Psalms 35:27	Proverbs 15:13	Psalms 122:1
Psalms 118:24	Matthew 9:2	Psalms 126:6
Proverbs 16:24	Proverbs 17:22	1 Peter 4:13
Acts 14:17		

Questions for Discussion

1. Define cheerfulness.
2. Why does guilt, fear, anxiety, depression, or jealousy destroy a cheerful heart?
3. How are you affected by a person who is continually gloomy and of a downcast spirit?
4. Name some ways to cheer the sad heart.
5. Is it sinful to develop a negative attitude?
6. What is a pessimist?
7. Name some steps a person must develop to possess a cheerful countenance.
8. How important is cheerfulness in winning souls for Christ?
9. Does a person possess a healthy, sound mind who lacks this beautiful quality?
10. What is your idea of mental health?
11. Why is it easy to be attracted to, and have faith in, a person of cheerful disposition?
12. Summarize the need, blessings and rewards of cheerfulness.

Suggested Assignment

1. Memorize Proverbs 17:22; Psalms 35:27.
2. Make sentences of the following words: cheerfulness, gloom, merry, rejoice, grouchy, downcast, depressing, glad.
3. Write a cheery note to some one who is ill or lonely.

Good Temper

"Let every man be quick to hear, slow to speak, slow to anger, for the anger of man does not work the righteousness of God" (James 1:19, 20).

Good temper might be defined as a disposition not easily provoked or irritated; a well-balanced mental disposition, especially with reference to the emotions; not quick to anger.

Other words which come to mind in connection with the thought of good temper are calmness and composure. Temper is both a native disposition and a matter of habit. Those people who are excitable by nature must strive to curb their emotions and bring them under control or they will become more pronounced, sometimes even leading to hysteria. Fortunately, temper is subject to self-control, so that even those persons who are born with an excitable nature may curb them to the point that they may have a good temper by habit. In most instances, it is not a lack of ability to control our emotions, but a lack of the desire to control them that causes us to "lose our temper," as it is commonly called. It seems easier at the moment to give way to our feelings and allow our temper to control us rather than to control our temper. We are deceived in this, however, as it takes us from the realm of freedom and denies us the power of reason.

"The toxin of fatigue has been demonstrated; but the poisons generated by evil temper and emotional excess over non-essentials have not yet been determined, although without a doubt they exist. Explosions of temper, emotional cyclones, and needless fear and panic over disease or misfortune that seldom materialize, are simply bad habits. By proper ventilation and illumination of the mind it is possible to cultivate tolerance, poise, and real courage. . . ." Elie Metchnikoff, the great biologist who penned these lines, would be gratified to know that what was a theory with him has become a proven fact. We now know that our emotions have a great effect upon us mentally, physically, and of course, spiritually.

Solomon, the man famed for his wisdom, wrote, "A wise man is cautious and turns away from evil, but a fool throws off restraint and is careless. A man of quick temper acts foolishly, but a man of discretion is patient" (Proverbs 14:16, 17). And in Proverbs 15:18, "A hot-tempered man stirs up strife, but he who is slow to anger quiets contention." He further warns, "Make no friendship with a man given to anger, nor go with a wrathful man, lest you learn his ways and entangle yourself in a snare" (Proverbs 22:24, 25).

The New Testament also warns us many times to practice self-control or good temper. To the Ephesians the apostle Paul wrote, "Let all bitterness and wrath and anger and clamor and slander be put away from you, with all malice, and be kind to one another, tenderhearted, forgiving one another, as God in Christ forgave you" (Ephesians 4:31, 32).

It is just as true today as when it was first written that a soft answer turns away wrath and grievous words stir up anger. There is no end to trouble, anger, harshness or violence. Each of these things calls for a reply in kind, and fuel is but added to the fire. The only way to meet anger is with kindness and the only way to meet harshness is with composure.

We can see the harm that a bad temper can have on us spiritually, mentally, and physically, and if we will carefully consider the facts we can hardly help agreeing with Robert Dodsley, the English publisher and poet, who said, "Consider how few things are worthy of anger, and you will wonder that any fools should be wroth." Since good temper can become a habit with us, we should strive daily to keep our emotions subject to our control.

Fill in Scriptures

1. _____A fool gives full vent to his anger, but a wise man quietly holds it back.

2. _____Be not quick to anger, for anger lodges in the bosom of fools.

3. _____Good sense makes a man slow to anger, and it is his glory to overlook an offense.

4._____But I say to you that everyone who is angry with his brother shall be liable to judgment; whoever insults his brother shall be liable to the council, and whoever says, 'You fool' shall be liable to the hell of fire.

5._____"But I say to you that hear, Love your enemies, do good to those who hate you, bless those who curse you, pray for those who abuse you."

6._____A soft answer turns away wrath, but a harsh word stirs up anger.

7._____Be angry but do not sin; do not let the sun go down on your anger.

8._____He who hates his brother is in the darkness and walks in the darkness, and does not know where he is going, because the darkness has blinded his eyes.

9._____Any one who hates his brother is a murderer, and you know that no murderer has eternal life.

10._____He who is slow to anger has great understanding but he who has a hasty temper exalts folly.

11._____It is better to live in a desert land than with a contentious and fretful woman.

Ecclesiastes 7:9	Proverbs 29:11	Proverbs 14:29
1 John 2:11	Luke 6:27, 28	Proverbs 21:19
1 John 3:15	Proverbs 19:11	Ephesians 4:26
Matthew 5:22	Proverbs 15:1	

Questions for Discussion

1. Define good temper.
2. Is a hasty temper the characteristic of a fool?
3. Have you ever seen good come from anger?
4. Is it always wrong to be angry?
5. What does anger often lead to?
6. How are we to behave around an angry person?
7. What is your boiling point?
8. What is your pet peeve?
9. Relate your last emotional cyclone and tell the effects of that storm.

10. How does one gain calmness, composure and self-control?

11. Summarize the need, blessings and rewards of a good temper.

Suggested Assignments

1. Memorize Proverbs 29:11.

2. Report on how Moses' anger prevented him from entering the promised land. Read Numbers 20:1-12.

3. Make sentences with the following words: anger, hate, vengeance, strife.

Preparation

The apostle Paul told Timothy to: "Do your best to present yourself to God as one approved, a workman who has no need to be ashamed, rightly handling the word of truth" (2 Timothy 2:15).

Preparation is defined as the act of making ready or fitting for a particular purpose; equipping, fitting as by study.

All of life consists in making preparation, and whatever our age, there is always something we can learn to better fit us for life. Indeed, this life we live in our mortal body is only a preparation for eternal life, and the WAY we live it determines WHERE we will spend eternity. How careful we should be to live each day in thoughtful, prayerful preparation, studying God's Word and working in his kingdom.

Preparation is also necessary for living a happier, fuller life here on earth. Joseph Appel wrote: "You want a better position than you now have in business, a better and fuller place in life. All right; think of that better place and you in it as already existing. Form the mental image. Keep on thinking of that higher position, keep the image constantly before you and—no, you will not suddenly be transported into the higher job, but you will find that you are **preparing** yourself to occupy the better position in life—your body, your energy, your understanding, your heart will all grow up to the job—and when you are ready, after hard work, after perhaps years of preparation, you will get the job and the higher place in life."

This is true of everything we might wish for. First we must have the goal, the mental image, before us, then we must set about preparing ourselves.

The higher our aims, our goals in life, the greater will be the need for preparation. For example, we would not trust anyone to doctor us in a serious illness who had not been schooled and prepared to become a qualified physician; nor should anyone else expect to "get by" in their chosen field without making due preparation.

It has been said, "Your sole contribution to the sum of things is yourself." We should make certain that our contribution will be something of value. We should begin NOW to make preparation.

Fill in Scriptures

1._____For which of you, desiring to build a tower, does not first sit down and count the cost, whether he has enough to complete it? Otherwise, when he has laid a foundation, and is not able to finish, all who see it begin to mock him, "This man began to build, and was not able to finish."

2._____Or what king, going to encounter another king in war, will not sit down first and take counsel whether he is able with ten thousand to meet him who comes against him with twenty thousand?

3._____Prepare to meet your God.

4._____Train up a child in the way he should go.

5._____Therefore you also must be ready; for the Son of Man is coming at an hour you do not expect.

6._____Be ready and keep ready.

7._____The bridegroom came, and those who were ready went in with him to the marriage feast; and the door was shut. Afterward the other maidens came also, saying, 'Lord, Lord, open to us,' but he replied, 'Truly, I say to you, I do not know you.' Watch therefore, for you know neither the day nor the hour.

8._____I advanced . . . beyond many of my own age among my people, so extremely zealous was I.

9._____Always be prepared to make a defense to any one who calls you to account for the hope that is in you, yet do it with gentleness and reverence.

10._____Make every effort to supplement your faith with virtue . . . knowledge . . . self-control . . . steadfastness . . . godliness . . . brotherly affection . . . For if these things are yours and abound, they keep you from being ineffective . . . For if you do this you will never fall.

11._____By reason of time you aught to be teachers.

12._____Put on the whole armour of God, that you may be able to stand against the wiles of the devil.

Hebrews 5:12 ASV	Proverbs 22:6	Galatians 1:14
Luke 14:28-30	Ezekiel 38:7	1 Peter 3:15
Amos 4:12	Matthew 24:44	2 Peter 1:5-10
Luke 14:31	Matthew 25:10-13	Ephesians 6:11

Questions for Discussion

1. Define preparation.
2. How did you prepare for today's class?
3. Are you adequately preparing yourself to advance the kingdom of Christ?
4. Can you give the complete rundown of Scripture that would inform one what to do to be saved?
5. Do you wish to marry someone who made no preparation for it?
6. What is involved in preparing one's self for a rich active service in Christ?
7. What do you feel that you could develop as your greatest talent or potential for the Lord?
8. Do you wish to lead the class in study or devotional on some occasion in the near future for approximately ten minutes?
9. Have you desires to become a full-time worker for the Lord?
10. Can you think of any worthy vocation that requires no preparation?
11. Besides time, effort and interest what are some other basic needs for one to prepare himself?
12. Summarize the need, blessings and rewards of preparation.

Suggested Assignments

1. Memorize 1 Peter 3:15, Hebrews 5:12
2. Make sentences with the following words: ready, qualify, slothful, negligent, preparation.
3. This week prayerfully search for one to bring to Bible class.

Loyalty

"Beloved, it is a loyal thing you do when you render any service to the brethren, especially to strangers" (3 John 5).

Loyalty may be defined as faithfulness to country, friend, promise, or duty; fidelty.

The first of our many duties in life is loyalty or fidelity. This is the quality of being faithful to our associates, friends, superiors, country, or any other to whom we owe allegiance. Loyalty suggests furthering the welfare and interests of those to whom we are obligated, and of defending their cause if need be.

History records many traitors; people despised because they were not loyal to their cause. In time of war the penalty is death; in ordinary times it is the loss of friendship and respect as well as a loss of self-respect, which is perhaps the hardest of all to live without. Society inflicts severe penalties upon those who violate the trusts reposed in them.

In the Bible we may read of the praise and promises to those who are loyal, and of the punishment to befall the unfaithful. The apostle wrote the Corinthians, "This is how one should regard us, as servants of Christ and stewards of the mysteries of God. Moreover it is required of stewards that they be found trustworthy," (1 Corinthians 4:1, 2). And to Titus he wrote, "Bid slaves to be submissive to their masters and to give satisfaction in every respect; they are not to be refractory, nor to pilfer, but to show entire and true fidelity, so that in everything they may adorn the doctrine of God our Savior" (Titus 2:9, 10).

Loyalty is a very praiseworthy and excellent virtue, one which we cannot afford to be without. It is also one which should not be too difficult for us to acquire, as, in most of us, our own conscience would forbid disloyalty. Therefore, if we will only think before speaking or acting we should not have to work too hard in order to make loyalty one of our characteristics.

Fill in Scriptures

1. _____If any man would come after me, let him deny himself and take up his cross and follow me. For whoever would save his life will lose it, and whoever loses his life for my sake will find it.

2. _____Not every one who says to me "Lord, Lord," shall enter the kingdom of heaven, but he who does the will of my Father who is in heaven.

3. _____But Balaam answered and said, ". . . though Balak were to give me his house full of silver and gold, I could not go beyond the command of the Lord my God."

4. _____Thomas, called the Twin, said to his fellow disciples, "Let also us go, that we may die with him."

5. _____"Entreat me not to leave you or to return from following you; for where you go I will go, and where you lodge I will lodge; your people shall be my people, and your God my God. Where you die I will die and there will I be buried."

6. _____But seek first his kingdom and his righteousness and all these things shall be yours as well.

7. _____"But now, if thou wilt forgive their sin—and if not, blot me, I pray thee, out of thy book which thou hast written."

8. _____So everyone who acknowledges me before me, I also will acknowledge before my Father who is in heaven; but whcever denies me before men, I also will deny before my Father who is in heaven.

9. _____Prove me, O Lord, and try me; test my heart and my mind.

10. _____And he said to them, "How is it that you sought me? Did you not know that I must be in my Father's house?"

11. _____Indeed I count everything as loss because of the surpassing worth of knowing Christ Jesus my Lord.

12._____For he nearly died for the work of Christ, risking his
life to complete your service to me.

13._____If we have died with him, we shall also live with him;
if we endure, we shall also reign with him.

Matthew 7:21	Matthew 6:33	Ruth 1:16-17
2 Timothy 2:11, 12	Matthew 16:24-25	Exodus 32:32
Psalms 26:2	Matthew 10:32-33	Numbers 22:18
Philippians 3:8	Philippians 2:30	Luke 2:49
John 11:16		

Questions for Discussion

1. Define loyalty.
2. Do you feel this is one of your strong characteristics?
3. Would you wish to be associated with, or be married to, or in business with, or active in any endeavor with a person who disregards loyalty?
4. How is loyalty tested?
5. How can one gain self-respect after being disloyal?
6. What affect has disloyalty on the conscience?
7. What is the price one must pay to be loyal to Christ?
8. How does the world, Satan, and the flesh, operate to spoil loyalty?
9. Can you think of Jesus without thinking of loyalty?
10. Have you avoided sacrifice, work, or full commitment?
11. Do you feel that the average member has courage to defend publicly his faith in Christ?
12. Do you feel that everyone in this class would be willing to live, die, pray and suffer for the kingdom of Christ?
13. How does one strengthen his loyalty?
14. How can we help each other to strengthen loyalty?
15. Is there anything that could cause you to deny Christ as the Son of God?
16. Can a person ever be called good or great without loyalty?
17. Summarize the need, blessings and rewards of loyalty.

Suggested Assignments

1. Memorize Matthew 10:32, 33.
2. Make sentences of the following words: treason; loyalty; deny; confess Christ; commitment.
3. Commend one whom you feel has developed an outstanding loyalty to Christ and His church.
4. Go out of your way to encourage one whom you feel is slipping or drifting from duty.

Humility

The apostle Paul wrote to the Philippians, "Do nothing from selfishness or conceit, but in humility count others better than yourselves" (Philippians 2:3).

Humility is the state or quality of being lowly in mind, unassuming, meek, unpretending, or modest.

Humility is a characteristic of the true Christian, one that the Lord has many times warned that we must have. It is not a natural quality with us, but one that we must strive to acquire.

Even apart from its value of helping to make us pleasing and acceptable to God, it is of great value in our dealings with our fellow man.

Humility prevents arrogance and pride, and will save us the embarrassment that comes to the boastful. The old proverb, "Pride goeth before a fall," is a truth that many boastful people have learned to their mortification.

Paul warned the Romans, "For by the grace given to me I bid everyone among you not to think of himself more highly than he ought to think" (Romans 12:3). If we are humble we will not think too highly of ourselves, but will consider other people and give them their proper respect. Let us develop humility in our lives and not over-value our importance in the world.

If one does not appreciate humility it will be impossible for him to properly serve others, or be acceptable in the sight of God. Humility is the root of love. The essence of love is selflessness. Love grows in the heart of one who empties himself. It is said of Jesus that He "emptied Himself." One must dethrone himself before he can truly love. Humility is true greatness. Abraham said, "Behold, I have taken upon myself to speak to the Lord, I who am but dust and

75

ashes." One must cultivate a spirit of poverty. Jesus said, "Blessed are the poor in spirit." The opposite of humility is pride, the greatest of all sins. It was pride that caused the devil to fall. He declared, "I will ascend to heaven; above the stars of God. I will set my throne on high; I will sit on the Mount of Assembly in the far north; I will ascend above the heights of the clouds; I will make myself like the Most High" (Isaiah 14:13-15 RSV). His self-importance brought ruin.

God hates a "proud look." One who is conceited, and self-important, filled with pride is in a complete anti-God state of mind. "He that exalts himself shall be debased," and "he who humbles himself shall be exalted." John the Baptist declared, "He must increase, but I must decrease" (John 3:30).

Fill in Scriptures

1. _____Humble yourselves therefore under the mighty hand of God that in due time he may exalt you.

2. _____Blessed are the poor in spirit, for theirs is the kingdom of heaven.

3. _____God opposes the proud, but gives grace to the humble.

4. _____I bid every one among you not to think of himself more highly than he ought to think.

5. _____The centurion answered him, "Lord, I am not worthy to have you come under my roof."

6. _____Whoever humbles himself like this child, he is the greatest in the kingdom.

7. _____He who is greatest among you shall be your servant; whoever exalts himself will be humbled, and whoever humbles himself will be exalted.

8. _____Do nothing from selfishness or conceit, but in humility count others better than yourselves.

9. _____The Pharisee stood and prayed thus with himself, "God, I thank thee that I am not like other men, extortioners, unjust, adulterers, or even like this tax collector. I fast twice a week, I give tithes of all that I get." But the tax collector, standing far off, would not even lift up his eyes to heaven, but beat his breast, saying, "God, be merciful to me a sinner!" I tell you, this man went

down to his house justified rather than the other.

10._____If I then, your Lord and Teacher, have washed your feet, you also ought to wash one another's feet. I have given you an example.

Luke 18:11-14   Romans 12:3   Matthew 8:8
James 4:6   Matthew 23:11   Matthew 5:3
Matthew 18:4   John 13:14-15   Philippians 2:3
1 Peter 5:6

Questions for Discussion

1. Define humility.
2. Why do some people exaggerate their own worth or importance?
3. Do some people, who gain much of this world's goods, develop a false financial pride that causes them to feel superior to others?
4. Explain how some may develop such a spiritual pride to the point that they feel superior to others.
5. How may one develop an intellectual pride and look down on others?
6. Can one's own physical beauty cause him or her to become proud?
7. "What have you that you did not receive? If then you received it, why do you boast as if it were not a gift?" (1 Corinthians 4:7). Discuss.
8. Why is it great to be like a child?
9. Explain how you feel in the presence of one who manifests an excessive display of self-esteem or arrogance.
10. Why do some people interpret humility as a sign of weakness?
11. Name some positive ways to develop humility.
12. Summarize the need, blessings and rewards of humility.

Suggested Assignments

1. Memorize Matthew 23:11; Romans 12:3.
2. Make sentences of the following words: proud, humility, ego, arrogance, meek.

3. Write a personal letter to God telling him of your weaknesses
    and need of help.

Courage

The apostle Paul told the Corinthians to "Be watchful, stand firm in your faith, be courageous, be strong" (1 Corinthians 16:13).

Courage is defined as bravery; boldness; fearlessness; that quality of spirit which faces danger without flinching.

It is in part a natural quality and partly a matter of the will. This quality is needed in our daily living, as it is courage that will enable us to do the right thing when doing something wrong would seem to afford more tempting rewards at the moment. Courage in daily life is even more common than it is on the battlefield. It is more important that we meet the difficulties of life courageously than it is to have courage to face the enemy in time of war. It is necessary when we have decisions to make concerning things which are new and strange to us, that we do so with thoughtfulness and fearlessness.

The American novelist James L. Allen said, "Whether you be man or woman you will never do anything in this world without courage. It is the greatest quality of the mind next to honor."

God would have his children be courageous and live lives that are holy and acceptable in his sight. We must have the courage not only to live the Christian life ourselves, but to do the Christian work of telling others of Christ our Savior. When Peter and John were being questioned by the Jewish high priest and his family they answered by preaching to them about Christ and salvation. "Now when they saw the boldness of Peter and John, and perceived that they were uneducated, common men, they wondered; and they recognized that they had been with Jesus" (Acts 4:13). It took courage for these men to preach to their accusers about Jesus when they had just been arrested for preaching about him to others.

We have all thrilled to stories of the men and women who have shown exceptional courage in the face of great odds; it is a trait which is admired by all. Nowhere will we find greater examples of courage than are to be found in the Bible. Stephen, the first Christian martyr, had the courage to preach to the mob about Jesus even though it cost him his life. The apostle Paul braved perils and persecution daily to teach others the way of salvation. Each of the apostles, and untold thousands of the early Christians, courageously gave their lives rather than turn from God. We do not have such perils to meet today in this country, but even here it takes courage to live the Christian life. In Hebrews 4:16 we read, "Let us then with confidence draw near to the throne of grace, that we may receive mercy and find grace to help in time of need." God will strengthen us in everything we do, if we will only have the courage to obey him.

Since this is a quality so vital to our welfare, let us determine to regulate our life according to the will of the Lord, then we will find we have courage enough to face any of life's problems.

Fill in Scriptures

1._____I will not fail you or forsake you. Be strong and of good courage.

2._____Therefore gird up your minds . . . set your hope fully upon the grace that is coming to you at the revelation of Jesus Christ.

3._____We know that in everything God works for good with those who love him.

4._____He gives power to the faint, and to him who has no might he increases strength. Even youths shall faint and be weary, and young men shall fall exhausted; but they who wait for the Lord shall renew their strength, they shall mount up with wings like eagles, they shall run and not be weary, they shall walk and not faint.

5._____He who is in you is greater than he who is in the world.

6._____Your servant has killed both lions and bears; and this uncircumcised Philistine shall be like one of them, seeing he has defied the armies of the living God.

7._____Be of good courage, and let us play the man for our people, and for the cities of our God; and may the Lord do what seems good to him.

8._____For he nearly died for the work of Christ, risking his life to complete your service.

9._____So they called them and charged them not to speak or teach at all in the name of Jesus. But Peter and John answered them, "Whether is it right in the sight of God to listen to you rather than to God, you must judge; for we cannot but speak of what we have seen and heard."

10._____And there we saw the Nephilim . . . and we seemed to ourselves like grasshoppers, and so we seemed to them.

11._____I can do all things in him who strengthens me.

12._____But as for the cowardly, the faithless, the polluted . . . and all liars, their lot shall be in the lake that burns with fire and brimstone, which is the second death.

13._____Even though I walk through the valley of the shadow of death, I will fear no evil; for thou art with me.

14._____But I do not account my life as any value nor precious to myself, if only I may accomplish my course and the ministry which I received from the Lord.

15._____Therefore lift your drooping hands and strengthen your weak knees.

Acts 20:24	Psalms 23:4	Revelation 21:8
Acts 4:18-20	Joshua 1:5-6	Philippians 2:30
Isaiah 40:29-31	Philippians 4:13	Numbers 13:33
Hebrews 12:12	2 Samuel 10:12	1 Samuel 17:36
1 John 4:4	1 Peter 1:13	Romans 8:28

Questions for Discussion

1. Define courage.
2. Why are some people cowardly?
3. Would you as Paul rather "die daily" than deny the Lord?
4. How much courage does it take to witness each week for Christ and give him your very best?
5. Is the untroubled, easy life the ideal?
6. Describe the most courageous person that you have ever met or read about.

7. Is there any more effective tool of Satan than discouragement?

8. How can we help one another to be more courageous?

9. What does it mean in Numbers 14:24, where it says that Caleb had a "different spirit"?

10. What, do you feel, are the most common fears of Christians?

11. Is courage a natural quality or one that is usually acquired through effort?

12. Are you ever silent when you should speak up for Christ and witness for him?

13. Are you courageous enough to put yourself into the hands of God and to be used anywhere?

14. Summarize the needs, blessings and rewards of courage.

Suggested Assignments

1. Memorize Acts 4:18-20; Philippians 4:13.

2. Make sentences of the following words: courage, fear, cowardly, strength, discouragement.

3. Make a three minute talk to your class on courage.

4. Commend someone whom you believe has acted in a very courageous way.

5. Knock on several doors giving invitations to your church assemblies.

Knowledge

The Apostle Peter, writing to Christians, exhorted, ". . . giving all diligence, add to your faith virtue; and to virtue knowledge. . ." (2 Peter 1:5 KJV).

Knowledge is a clear understanding of a truth or fact; the act or state of knowing; that which has been perceived or grasped mentally; learning.

There are many things which we need to have a knowledge of, but a knowledge of God's Word is the most important thing we can know. Jesus said, "You search the scriptures, because you think that in them you have eternal life; and it is they that bear witness to me" (John 5:39). If we did not have a knowledge of His Word, we could not know about the Lord and so could not have the hope of salvation which is promised to the obedient Christian.

We also need a knowledge concerning the important affairs of life, especially as related to the sphere we occupy, and that which we desire to attain. It is highly important that the individual possess a great deal of information concerning the great achievements of mankind, but it is of still greater importance that we have complete and exact knowledge regarding the details and requirements of our own vocation or calling.

There are several ways of gaining knowledge, and our printed pages contain the knowledge gained through hundreds of years of experience by mankind. Here we may feast upon the choicest morsels of human experience and gratify our desire for knowledge in a wholesome and profitable manner. Charles Kingsley, the British novelist, poet and social reformer, said: "Except a living man there is nothing more wonderful than a book; a message to us from the dead—from human souls we never saw, who lived perhaps thousands of miles away. And yet these—in those little sheets of paper, speak to us, arouse us, terrify us, teach us, comfort us, open their hearts to us as brothers." Yes, it has been truly said that "books are the ever-burning lamps of accumulated wisdom."

Another way of gaining knowledge is through our own personal experience. This, of course, will be somewhat limited when compared with the knowledge we may gain from the recorded experiences of others.

Acquiring knowledge is a habit which we should form as early as possible. Fortunately, good literature is available to all of us through our public libraries, and we should take advantage of this wonderful opportunity to build up a rich storehouse of learning. Henry Wadsworth Longfellow expressed a great truth well when he said, "An enlightened mind is not hoodwinked; it is not shut up in a gloomy prison till it thinks the walls of its own dungeon the limits of the universe, and the reach of its own chain the outer verge of intelligence."

Fill in Scriptures

1. _____A fool takes no pleasure in understanding, but only in expressing his opinion.

2. _____But in your hearts reverence Christ as Lord. Always be prepared to make a defense to any one who calls you to account for the hope that is in you.

3. _____But grow in the grace and knowledge of our Lord and Savior.

4. _____My people are destroyed for lack of knowledge.

5. _____Wise men lay up knowledge but the babbling of a fool brings ruin near.

6. _____Happy is the man who finds wisdom and the man who gets understanding.

7. _____All Scripture is inspired by God and profitable for teaching, for reproof, for correction, and for training in righteousness, that the man of God may be complete, equipped for every good work.

8. _____Anyone who goes ahead and does not abide in the doctrine of Christ does not have God.

9. _____His delight is in the law of the Lord, and on his law he

meditates day and night.

10._____And you will know the truth, and the truth will make you free.

11._____Give me understanding that I may live.

12._____The word that I have spoken will be his judge on the last day.

Proverbs 18:2   2 Peter 3:18   2 Timothy 3:16, 17
Psalms 119:144   1 Peter 3:15   Proverbs 10:14
Psalms 1:2   Hosea 4:6   Proverbs 3:13
2 John 9   John 8:32   John 12:48

Questions for Discussion

1. Define knowledge.

2. Do you feel that gaining biblical knowledge is one of your strong characteristics?

3. What are some obstacles, hindrances, or temptations one must overcome in order to acquire full knowledge of God's will?

4. How is one to sift out the major truths from the minor?

5. Can you give Bible Scriptures for what one must do to be saved?

6. How much time on an average do you spend each week reading the Bible?

7. Can one be mentally, as well as physically, lazy?

8. Abraham Lincoln said that he didn't think much of the man who is not wiser today than yesterday; do you agree?

9. Will knowledge help us to do all things well?

10. Have you made excuses for failing to study and prepare lessons?

11. What is the price one must pay to gain much knowledge?

12. What part does lack of knowledge play in establishing the many false doctrines and false religions?

13. Summarize the need, blessings and rewards of gaining biblical knowledge.

86

Suggested Assignments

1. Memorize Proverbs 18:2; 1 Peter 3:15.
2. Present a three-minute talk to the class.
3. Arise fifteen minutes earlier than usual each day this week to study the Bible.
4. Make sentences of the following words: knowledge, ignorance, truth, understanding.

Good Workmanship

From Solomon, the man of wisdom, come these words, "Whatever your hand finds to do, do it with your might; for there is no work or thought or knowledge or wisdom in Sheol, to which you are going" (Ecclesiastes 9:10).

Good workmanship is defined as being above average in the skill and methods of a workman; the efficient execution of, finish, or quality of anything made; the product of skill and labor.

A person's work is usually regarded as an expression of his or her personality. A careless and indifferent man cannot turn out a good piece of work; his habits of carelessness are certain to show themselves. Real accomplishment costs trouble, thought and labor. Good workmanship in any field is almost certain to indicate some good quality, or often several of them, in the worker.

There are few pleasures that can compare with that we get from creating something. It is a pleasure that can't be measured by the amount of money or fame the product will bring, but is in the form of pride of accomplishment; the knowledge that we have given to our work the best of our ability and have created something that would not exist except for our efforts. It is a personal taste of victory that comes only after we have actually done our best; for if we haven't done quite as well as we could have, we lose the sense of exultation that comes from putting our utmost into our work.

The apostle Paul told Timothy to do his best to present himself to God as one approved, "A workman who has no need to be ashamed, rightly handling the word of truth" (2 Timothy 2:15). And to the Ephesians Paul wrote that we are God's workmanship, "created in Christ Jesus for good works, which God prepared beforehand, that we should walk in them" (Ephesians 2:10).

It is God's will that we work, and that our workmanship be good. While our best efforts are required to bring any great amount of success in this world, it might be possible to "get by" among men without their realizing that we are not doing our best, but God knows our abilities and whether or not we could do better. Remember, only our best can be termed "good workmanship" with God.

Fill in Scriptures

1. _____ And every work that he undertook in the service of the house of God and in accordance with the law and the commandments, seeking his God, he did with all his heart, and prospered.

2. _____ Whatever your hand finds to do, do it with your might.

3. _____ His master said to him, "Well done, good and faithful servant; you have been faithful over little, I will set you over much; enter into the joy of your master."

4. _____ So that you may not be sluggish, but imitators of those who through faith and patience inherit the promises.

5. _____ I know your works, your love and faith and service and patient endurance, and that your latter works exceed the first.

6. _____ Be steadfast, immovable, always abounding in the work of the Lord, knowing that in the Lord your labor is not in vain.

7. _____ Let your light so shine before men, that they may see your good works and give glory to your Father who is in heaven.

8. _____ Behold, I am coming . . . to repay every one for what he has done.

9. _____ You wicked and slothful servant . . . And cast the worthless servant into outer darkness; there men will weep and gnash their teeth.

10. _____ See that you excel in this gracious work also.

11. _____ Many women have done excellently, but you surpass them all.

12. _____ Now if anyone builds on the foundation with gold,

silver, precious stones, wood, hay, stubble—each man's work will become manifest, for the Day will disclose it, because it will be revealed with fire and the fire will test what sort of work each one has done.

Ecclesiastes 9:10	1 Corinthians 15:58	Revelations 22:12
1 Corinthians 3:12-13	2 Corinthians 8:7	Proverbs 31:29
Matthew 25:21	Revelation 2:19	Matthew 5:16
2 Chronicles 31:21	Hebrews 6:12	Matthew 25:26-30

Questions for Discussion

1. Define good workmanship.
2. Do you feel that is one of your strong characteristics?
3. Would you wish to be united in marriage, or business, or any endeavor with those who thought little of good workmanship?
4. How does one attain good working habits?
5. Can you name any worthwhile endeavor where it is not needed?
6. How does God look upon inferior workmanship?
7. What effect does indifference, slothfulness and carelessness have upon one's employer, teacher, or society in general?
8. Is it safe to assume that many products have spoiled and sales been lost because of poor services rendered?
9. How soon should one be discharged by his employer because of unsatisfactory labor?
10. Is good workmanship a premium in the church?
11. What makes a person lazy?
12. Have church programs gone defunct because of neglect and carelessness?
13. Why do some people seem inperceptible to proper standards of workmanship?
14. Are we derelict in duty if we fail to commend good workmanship?
15. Do you feel that the old attitude that "anything is good enough" is too prevalent in church activities? Why?
16. What is the price to pay for good workmanship?
17. How can all Christians be made aware of the need for good

workmanship?

18. Summarize the need, blessings, and rewards of good workmanship.

Suggested Assignments

1. Memorize 2 Timothy 2:15; 2 Chronicles 31:21.
2. Commend someone who has done a job well.
3. Make sentences of the following words: lazy; carelessness; diligence; slothfulness; shirk; thoroughness.

Ideality

The apostle Paul wrote the Ephesian brethren, "Put off your old nature which belongs to your former manner of life and is corrupt through deceitful lusts, and be renewed in the spirit of your minds, and put on the new nature, created after the likeness of God in true righteousness and holiness" (Ephesians 4:22-24).

Ideality is the capacity to create mental images of things in their perfection, or as they should be, rather than as they are; the quality or state of seeking things in their beauty or excellence.

Among our mental qualities is the power or capacity to form ideals. It depends upon our imagination and is, in reality, one of its phases or branches. This is known as "ideality." An ideal is a mental picture of a state of being, or of a quality or a combination of qualities not yet realized but which appeals to one as desirable and worthy of attainment or imitation.

Ideals come from within ourselves but are affected, or directed, by the things we learn. Thus we see that if we are to have high ideals we must take care to train ourselves to admire and seek those things which are good, and worthy of attainment. This will be easier for us if we are first careful of our environment: our friends and associates, the kind of talk we listen to, the books we read, and most of all the things we let our minds dwell on. The Philippians received this exhortation from the apostle Paul, "Finally, brethren, whatever is true, whatever is honorable, whatever is just, whatever is pure, whatever is lovely, whatever is gracious, if there is any excellence, if there is anything worthy of praise, think about these things" (Philippians 4:8).

It has been said, "Ideals are like stars; you will not succeed in touching them with your hands, but like the seafaring men on the

92

desert of waters, you choose them as your guides, and following them, you reach your destiny.''

Let us gravely consider our ideals, to make and keep them as worthwhile goals to steer our lives toward. Most of all, though, let us always keep before us the ideal of the fruitful, obedient Christian life.

Fill in Scriptures

1. _____And Peter said, "Lo, we have left our homes and followed you." And (Jesus) said to them, "Truly I say to you, there is no man who has left house or wife or brothers or parents or children for the sake of the Kingdom of God, who will not receive manifold more in this time, and in the age to come eternal life."

2. _____Be imitators of me, as I am of Christ.

3. _____For to this you have been called, because Christ also suffered for you, leaving you an example, that you should follow in his steps.

4. _____You, therefore, must be perfect, as your heavenly Father is perfect.

5. _____I know O Lord, that the way of man is not in himself, that it is not in man who walks to direct his steps.

6. _____Follow the example of the faith which our Father Abraham had.

7. _____Indeed I count everything as loss because of the surpassing worth of knowing Christ Jesus my Lord. For his sake I have suffered the loss of all things, and count them as refuse, in order that I may gain Christ.

8. _____And all who believed were together and had all things in common; and they sold their possessions and goods and distributed them to all, as any had need. And day by day, attending the temple together and breaking bread in their homes, they partook of food with glad and generous hearts, praising God and having favor with all the people. And the Lord added to their number day by day those who were being saved.

1 Corinthians 11:1 1 Peter 2:21 Jeremiah 10:23
Acts 2:44-47 Matthew 5:48 Romans 4:12
Luke 18:28-30 Philippians 3:8

Questions for Discussion

1. Define ideality.
2. Why is it wise to continually keep before us the highest ideals?
3. How can we account for the early church having and keeping such a high standard of perfection—even total surrender!
4. Why is it good to write down on paper and tell others of our ideals and goals?
5. Are we apt to reach our ideals and conform perfectly to the exact mental image that we have written down?
6. Name several normal obstacles to reaching goals.
7. Why is it wise to keep the highest possible standards before us even if it is impossible to complete them perfectly?
8. What are some of your immediate and long-range goals for Christ?
9. What is the ultimate of all goals possible?
10. How can we help each other reach desired goals?
11. Summarize the need, blessings, and rewards of ideality.

Suggested Assignments

1. Memorize 1 Peter 2:21; Philippians 3:8.
2. If possible, relate to class your immediate and your long-range goals for Christ and his church.

Good Speech

From the wisdom of Solomon comes this simile: "A word fitly spoken is like apples of gold in pictures of silver" (Proverbs 25:11 KJV).

Good speech might be defined as the expression of thought in well chosen words.

People are judged by the words they speak, as well as the things they do, for these are the only things we have by which to know the mind or heart of others. Seneca, the Roman philosopher who lived in the time of Christ said, "Speech is the index of the mind." And Christ himself said, "Out of the abundance of the heart the mouth speaks" (Matthew 12:34).

Not many of us can be great orators swaying multitudes by our words, but we can learn to speak in such a way that those few who do hear us will receive words carefully chosen to convey the true meaning of the thought we are seeking to impart. It was the belief of Franklin D. Roosevelt that good speech consists of using the simplest word that will express the thought, and his speech was admired throughout the nation.

Unfortunately, many people, even in their daily conversations, seem to feel that they must use the longest or least familiar words they can master in order that their audience will consider them intelligent. Actually this only serves to defeat their purpose, making it difficult for some to understand them, and causing others to consider them "Show-offs." This does not mean that long or less familiar words have no place in our vocabularly, because the more words we know the more we have to choose from. It does mean, however, that in choosing them we should make certain they will better express the exact shade of meaning we wish to convey. As

95

the apostle Paul asked the Corinthians, "If you in a tongue utter speech that is not intelligible, how will any one know what is said?" (1 Corinthians 14:9). He, of course, was referring to the miraculous gift of speaking in tongues, but the same thing would apply to us if we speak in words our hearers cannot understand. It shows how futile our speech would be.

In the Ephesian letter we read, "Let no evil talk come out of your mouths, but only such as is good for edifying, as fits the occasion, that it may impart grace to those who hear. And do not grieve the Holy Spirit of God, in whom you were sealed for the day of redemption" (Ephesians 4:29-30). God would have his children give careful thought to the things they say, and there are many admonitions in His Word to this affect. In Proverbs 29:30 we read, "Do you see a man who is hasty in his words? There is more hope for a fool than for him." And in Matthew 12:36, 37, "I tell you, on the day of judgment men will render account for every careless word they utter; for by your words you will be justified, and by your words you will be condemned."

Since the way we speak is so important in making our thoughts known, and others will see us in the light of our words, it is necessary that we learn to speak as well as possible. Most of all, however, we must keep in mind that the Lord knows the way we speak, and that we will have to give account of our words.

Fill in Scriptures

1._____Fine speech is not becoming to a fool.

2._____Let your speech always be gracious, seasoned with salt.

3._____. . . man who is perverse in speech, and is a fool.

4._____Death and life are in the power of the tongue.

5._____By the blessings of the upright a city is exalted, but it is overthrown by the mouth of the wicked.

6._____The tongue is a fire.

7._____. . . and sound speech that cannot be condemned.

8._____Let what you say be simply Yes or No; anything more than this comes from evil.

9._____He that would love life and see good days let him keep his tongue from evil and his lips from speaking guile.

10._____A time to keep silence and a time to speak.

11._____I tell you, on the day of Judgment men will render account for every careless word they utter.

12._____Let everyone speak the truth with his neighbor.

13._____Let every man be quick to hear, slow to speak.

14._____Do not speak evil against one another, brethren.

15._____If anyone thinks he is religious and does not bridle his tongue but deceives his heart, this man's religion is vain.

16._____These are grumblers, malcontents. . . loud-mouthed boasters, flattering people to gain advantage.

17._____A gentle tongue is a tree of life.

18._____And so spoke that a great company believed, both Jews and of Greeks.

19._____Their throat is an open grave.

20._____Let the words of my mouth and the meditation of my heart be acceptable in thy sight.

21._____. . . who whet their tongues like swords, who aim bitter words like arrows.

22._____Even before a word is on my tongue, lo, O Lord, thou knowest it altogether.

23._____Soft answer turns away wrath, but a harsh word stirs up anger.

Proverbs 17:7	Proverbs 19:1	1 Peter 3:10
Titus 2:8 ASV	James 3:6	Matthew 12:36
Proverbs 18:21	Matthew 5:37	James 1:19
Colossians 4:6	Ephesians 4:25	Romans 3:13
Ecclesiastes 3:7	James 1:26	Psalms 64:3
James 4:11	Proverbs 15:4	Psalms 139:4
Jude 16	Psalms 19:14	Proverbs 15:1
Acts 14:1	Proverbs 11:11	

Questions for Discussion

1. Define good speech.
2. Do you feel that it is one of your strong characteristics?
3. Why do people use slang or boisterous language?
4. Would you wish to ever be associated with those who disregard

good speech?

5. Should some tongues be registered as a dangerous weapon?
6. What did Jesus mean when he said that by our words we shall be justified or condemned? (Matthew 12:36, 37).
7. Jesus said in Matthew 12:34, "Out of the abundance of the heart the mouth speaks." Could there ever be an exception to this?
8. Are words always a copy of the heart?
9. Why do men curse?
10. Why are words spoken in anger most often regretted?
11. What are: "Idle words?" "Words seasoned with salt?"
12. Relate the effects of **negative** and **positive** conversations.
13. Explain the meaning of: harsh words; seductive words; words of flattery; subtle words; sarcastic words; deceitful words; curse words.
14. Explain how words can be like switches that turn on great dynamoes or create verbal cyclones or emotional tornadoes.
15. Explain how life and death are in the power of the tongue.
16. Is silence always golden?
17. Summarize needs, blessings and rewards of good speech.

Suggested Assignments

1. Memorize Proverbs 18:21; Proverbs 15:1; Proverbs 6:16-19; Matthew 12:36, 37.
2. Go all week without uttering one word of complaint, murmuring, or criticism.
3. Make sentences of the following words: anger; slang; tongue; nagging.
4. Report on negative and positive conversations heard the passed week and their effects.
5. Speak some encouraging words to someone this week.

Self-Reliance

From the pen of the apostle Paul we read, "Let each one test his own work, and then his reason to boast will be in himself alone and not in his neighbor. For each man will have to bear his own load" (Galatians 6:4, 5).

Self-reliance is defined as reliance on, or confidence in, one's own ability, efforts, or judgment.

This does not mean that we can ever be completely self-sufficient. Far from it! We are all dependent upon others, and must learn to work with them as effectively and pleasantly as possible. Most of all, we are dependent upon God, and it is only through his grace and mercy that we live. It does mean, however, that there is a work for each of us and that we must learn to do everything of which we are capable to take our place in the world as a useful citizen, and not to rely on others to shoulder the responsibilities that are ours.

When we are young we are almost totally dependent upon others, relying upon them for shelter, food, care and other necessities, but as we grow older in years we also grow more and more self-reliant, learning to do many things for ourselves.

Self-reliance is, when you think of it, really the mark of maturity in an individual. Those who fail to grow in this quality can never take their place in the world, which is the desire of every mature person. Whatever we wish to get from the world in the way of a place to serve, in the way of riches, influence or pleasure, will only come when we go after it depending upon our own resources as the means of obtaining it. We can receive help and encouragement from others, but the way we live our life depends upon us and our own resourcefulness.

Paul exhorted the Philippians to "work out your own salvation with fear and trembling; for God is at work in you, both to will and to work for his good pleasure" (Philippians 2:12, 13). And in Philippians 4:13, "I can do all things in him who strengthens me." This does not mean that we can do just anything that we might find pleasing to ourselves and be of service to God, but that we should obey his commands and do our part in taking the gospel of Christ to the lost. This is our work and we cannot rely upon others to do it for us, but if we are faithful to his commands we have the spirit of Christ dwelling in us and he will strengthen us.

Let each of us heed the words of Paul and "test" our own work "for each man will have to bear his own load." This growth in self-reliance will enable us to mature into useful citizens of the world, and into useful citizens of God's kingdom.

Fill in Scriptures

1. _____Our sufficiency is from God.

2. _____Ask and it will be given you; seek, and you will find; knock and it will be opened to you.

3. _____I can do all things in him who strengthens me.

4. _____In the fear of the Lord one has strong confidence.

5. _____The Lord is the Strength of his people.

6. _____. . . in whom we have boldness and confidence of access through our faith in him.

7. _____We know that in everything God works for good with those who love him.

8. _____We are more than conquerors through him who loved us.

9. _____And my God will supply every need of yours.

10. _____My grace is sufficient for you.

11. _____Therefore lift your drooping hands and strengthen your weak knees.

12. _____We seemed to ourselves like grasshoppers.

13. _____Then David said to the Philistines, "You come to me with a sword and with a spear and with a javelin; but I come to you in the name of the Lord."

14. _____But to all who received him, . . . he gave power to become children of God.

15. _____I will be with you; I will not fail you. . . be strong and of good courage.

16. _____He who believes in me will also do the works that I do; and greater works than these will he do.

17. _____If God is for us, who is against us.

18. _____The Lord is my light and my salvation; whom shall I fear?

19. _____The Lord is my shepherd, I shall not want.

20. _____Be strong in the Lord and in the strength of his might.

Romans 8:28	Ephesians 6:10	Philippians 4:13
Philippians 4:19	Romans 8:31	Joshua 1:5-6
John 1:12	2 Corinthians 3:5	Psalms 27:1
Matthew 7:7	2 Corinthians 12:9	1 Samuel 17:45
Psalms 28:8	John 14:12	Hebrews 12:12
Romans 8:37	Ephesians 3:12	Numbers 13:33
Psalms 23:1	Proverbs 14:26	

Questions for Discussion

1. Define self-reliance.
2. Do you feel this is one of your strong characteristics?
3. Will self-reliance help you to do all things well?
4. Would you wish to be married to, or associated with, those who have no self-reliance?
5. Does self-reliance mean in any way that we are not dependent upon God?
6. How does one build self-reliance or confidence?
7. Is self-reliance contrary to humility?
8. What is the difference between being self-reliant and being self-sufficient?
9. Are we not all very dependent upon God and each other?
10. Can we have courage without self-reliance?
11. What is your estimate of the average Christian? Is he confident, courageous, self-reliant, with a positive attitude—believing in

victory?

12. How can we help one another to be more self-reliant?

13. Summarize the needs, blessings, and rewards of self-reliance.

Suggested Assignments

1. Memorize Philippians 4:13; Romans 8:28.

2. Report on what you feel you are most capable of doing well for the Lord.

3. Study and report on the entire chapter of Numbers 13.

4. Take notes on the preacher's sermon.

5. Prayerfully consider someone whom you shall endeavor to bring to your Bible class.

6. Either by letter or in person commend one whom you believe is most reliant and has proven himself to be a courageous servant of Christ.

Industrious

". . . If any one will not work, let him not eat. For we hear that some of you are living in idleness, mere busybodies, not doing any work. Now such persons we command and exhort in the Lord Jesus Christ to do their work in quietness and to earn their own living" (2 Thessalonians 3:10-12).

Industry is a steady application to a task, business, or labor; hard and consistent work.

Without industry one cannot expect to accomplish anything worthwhile, however many talents he may possess. No amount of brilliancy or training will overcome a lack of industry. Julian Ralph, the American author and newspaper reporter, said, "I do not despise genius—indeed, I wish I had a basketful of it instead of a brain, but yet, after a great deal of experience and observation, I have become convinced that being industrious is a better horse to ride than genius. It may never carry any one man as far as genius has carried individuals, but industry—patient, steady, intelligent industry—will carry thousands into comfort and even into celebrity, and this it does with absolute certainty; whereas genius often refuses to be tamed and managed, and often goes with wretched morals. If you are to wish for either, wish for industry."

Someone has said that action is life; inaction, death. Perhaps this is why industry is so essential in achieving success. Busy people are usually happy, and conversely, happy people are usually busy. A great deal of life's joys consists in doing to the best of one's ability everything one attempts to do. There is a sense of satisfaction and pride in looking back over a work well done which the careless worker can never know.

To achieve success in this world a person must attend strictly to business. The one reaching the top is the one who is not content with doing just what is required, but does more. Andrew Carnegie said, "I congratulate poor young men upon being born to that ancient and honorable degree which renders it necessary that they should devote themselves to hard work."

In order that we may form the habit of working industriously, let each of us do every task that we have, to the very best of our ability. In so doing we will be heeding the admonition of Paul to the Thessalonians: "We exhort you, brethren, . . . to aspire to live quietly, to mind your own affairs, and to work with your hands, as we charged you; so that you may command the respect of outsiders, and be dependent on nobody" (1 Thessalonians 4:10-12).

Fill in Scriptures

1._____Never flag in zeal, be aglow with the Spirit, serve the Lord.

2._____Well done, good and faithful servant; you have been faithful over a little, I will set you over much.

3_____Do you see a man skillful in his work? He will stand before kings; he will not stand before obscure men.

4._____For we hear that some of you are living in idleness, mere busybodies, not doing any work.

5._____We must work the works of him who sent me, while it is day; night comes, when no one can work.

6._____Now as you excel in everything—in faith, in utterance, in knowledge, in all earnestness, and in your love for us—see that you excel in this gracious work also.

7._____Be steadfast, immovable, always abounding in the work of the Lord, knowing that in the Lord your labor is not in vain.

8._____But Jesus answered them, "My Father is working still and I am working."

9._____Aspire to live quietly, to mind your own affairs, and to work with your hands, as we charged you.

10._____Work out your salvation with fear and trembling.

11._____Do you want to be shown, you foolish fellow, that faith apart from works is barren?

12._____For they gave . . . beyond their means . . . first they
        gave themselves.

13._____Because you are lukewarm, and neither cold or hot,
        I will spew you out of my mouth.

Matthew 25:21   2 Corinthians 8:3-5   John 5:17
James 2:20   Romans 12:11   Proverbs 22:29
John 9:4   2 Thessalonians 3:11   2 Corinthians 8:7
Philippians 2:12   Revelation 3:16   1 Thessalonians 4:11
1 Corinthians 15:58

Questions for Discussion

1. Define Industry.
2. Do you believe that it is one of your strong characteristics?
3. Do you wish to have as your close friends those who disregard this characteristic?
4. Will this quality help one to do all things well?
5. How are you involved for Christ?
6. What is God's attitude toward the non-involved?
7. What does it mean to go the "second mile"?
8. Explain what it means to seek the kingdom first.
9. Are most of us tending to the Lord's business as well as we should?
10. What do you feel is your greatest achievement for the Lord?
11. How can we help others to become more industrious?
12. Do you speak to someone each week hoping to interest them in Christ?
13. How many souls have been saved during the last twelve months by your congregation?
14. To each of the seven churches of Asia the Lord said, "I know your works." How should this impress us?
15. Summarize the need, blessing, and rewards of industry.

Suggested Assignment

1. Memorize 1 Corinthians 15:58; Matthew 6:33; Romans 12:11.
2. Bring a visitor to worship next Lord's day.

3. Give a report to class on all the programs of the church where you attend that are designed to build its self up; and also those that are designed to save the lost.

4. Make a list of the benevolent programs of the church.

5. Get an estimate from your leaders of approximate monies spent for evangelism last year.

6. Commend someone this week whom you know to be deeply involved in Christ's kingdom.

Discernment

And Solomon said, "Give thy servant therefore an understanding mind to govern thy people, that I may discern between good and evil; for who is able to govern this thy great people?" It pleased the Lord that Solomon had asked this. And God said to him, "Because you have asked this, and have not asked for yourself long life or riches or the life of your enemies, but have asked for yourself understanding to discern what is right, behold, I now do according to your word. Behold, I give you a wise and discerning mind, so that none like you has been before you and none like you shall arise after you" (1 Kings 3:9-12).

Discernment is clearness in judgment; penetration; insight; the power of distinguishing; faculty of nice or exact judgment.

It is highly important before making a decision that we be informed on all details pertaining to the matter under consideration. Then, from our experience and the facts at hand, we use our discernment, or judgment, in order to make the right decision. It is most important that we develop skill in this connection, as all during life we are continuously sitting as a judge upon matters which will vitally affect us.

Not a day, and scarcely an hour, of our life will pass that we will not have some decision to make, and our success will depend largely upon our ability to make the right choice. For example, we must use our judgment, or discernment, in selecting our friends and associates, the kind of work we intend to devote our life to, where we are to live, whom (or if) we are to marry, and even the everyday matters of what we are to eat and wear. In fact, even the most ordinary and commonplace matters of life call for us to make some sort of a choice, or decision, and we must exercise

108

care to discern the best if we are to have a happy and profitable life.

It is God's will that we use our powers of discernment to the very best of our ability, and there are many excellent examples of good judgment recorded in the Bible.

Jesus warned the Jews, "Do not judge by appearances, but judge with right judgment" (John 7:24). Sometimes a thing may appear to be one thing on the surface, and quite another upon closer and more careful examination. Taking time to give thoughtful attention to all of the facts may seem tiresome at first, but eventually, with practice, will become a habit that will do much toward enabling us to have a wonderfully successful life.

Fill in Scriptures

1. _____My son, give me your heart, and let your eyes observe my ways.

2. _____For anyone who eats and drinks without discerning the body eats and drinks judgment upon himself.

3. _____And no wonder, for even Satan disguises himself as an angel of light.

4. _____For false Christs and false prophets will arise and show great signs and wonders, so as to lead astray, if possible, even the elect.

5. _____Beloved, do not believe every spirit, but test the spirits to see whether they are of God; for many false prophets have gone out into the world.

6. _____Having the eyes of your hearts enlightened, that you may know what is the hope to which he has called you, what are the riches of his glorious inheritance in the saints, and what is the immeasurable greatness of his power in us who believe.

7. _____Open my eyes, that I may behold wondrous things out of thy law.

8. _____Go to this people, and say, "You shall indeed hear but never understand, and you shall indeed see but never perceive. For this people's heart has grown dull, and their ears are heavy of hearing, and their eyes they have closed."

9._____Who has bewitched you, before whose eyes Jesus Christ was publicly portrayed. . . ?

10._____Now these Jews were more noble than those in Thessalonica, for they received the word with all eagerness, examining the scriptures daily to see if these things were so.

11._____About this we have much to say which is hard to explain, since you have become dull of hearing.

12._____As it is written, "God gave them a spirit of stupor, eyes that should not see and ears that should not hear.

13._____Therefore God sends upon them a strong delusion, to make them believe what is false.

2 Corinthians 11:14 Proverbs 23:26 Acts 17:11
Matthew 24:24 1 Corinthians 11:29 Galatians 3:1
Romans 11:8 Psalms 119:18 1 John 4:1
2 Thessalonians 2:11 Hebrews 5:11 Acts 28:26-27
Ephesians 1:18-19

Questions for Discussion

1. Define discernment.

2. Do you feel that this is one of your strong characteristics?

3. Will discernment help one to do all things well?

4. Why did God give to some eyes of stupor?

5. In what ways can imaginative vision be a great asset to the church?

6. How can well-intentioned people lacking in keen perception create problems?

7. How can depth of perception be a great blessing or asset to teacher and student alike?

8. Should we not admire one who has a searching mind?

9. How has superfical observation and lack of discernment affected Christianity?

10. How does one train himself to possess insight or depth of discernment?

11. How can prejudice, tradition, emotion or hearsay spoil discernment?

12. Can you think of any vocation that does not require a good amount of discernment?

13. What person is most likely to grasp or comprehend what is obscure to others?

14. Summarize the need, blessings, and rewards of discernment.

Suggested Assignments

1. Memorize 1 Corinthians 11:28, 29; Proverbs 23:26.

2. Report on Acts 16:25-34. Point out how Paul's keen discernment saved a man from both physical and spiritual death.

3. Study prayerfully through the week to learn possible ways to help improve your Bible class or some other facet of church activities. Make suggestions to your teacher.

Foresight

"A prudent man foreseeth the evil, and hideth himself: but the simple pass on, and are punished" (Proverbs 22:3 KJV).

Foresight is the power or act of seeing in advance; heedful, thought for the future; prudence; prevision, forethought, or care.

The person who practices foresight will miss many of life's troubles. It is a mark of prudence to give thoughtful consideration to one's future, and the earlier we begin to make preparation for it the more successful we are likely to be. Unfortunately, too many people fail to realize the importance of study and growth in the habits that will contribute most to a happy and profitable future.

The time to make preparation is before we must meet the responsibilities of life, but it takes foresight to realize this. Parents and teachers try to impress children with this need, and to present the lessons to them that will lay the foundations for success. The young people who can foresee their need for education are the ones who will benefit most by it, and will go on to a worthwhile adult life.

In becoming a Christian we are exercising foresight, because we are hoping, planning, and working for a heavenly home. So, while it is a virtue that will help us throughout our life here, it is absolutely necessary if we are to have salvation. We may be sure that no one will be saved who does not want to be and does not have the foresight to prepare for it.

No man lives long enough or ever becomes wise enough to learn all the answers on his own. In fact, "the wisest man in the world is only picking up a few grains of sand on an infinite beach." Therefore, in order for one to have foresight he must gain help from others. The smart person will listen and learn from the experience of others and accept wise counseling. "There is nothing new under the sun"

112

(Ecclesiastes 1:9 RSV). Others have long ago traveled the road before us.

The one who goes blindly down the path of life unprepared for the future will certainly take the wrong cross roads and have much to regret. Some of the saddest words ever spoken are "they wouldn't listen." Those who trust to chance will follow the haphazard course and will, no doubt, fail in the end. It is obvious to all that, "You do not know about tomorrow" (James 4:14); yet we can prepare ourselves for it. "Thou will show me the path of life" (Psalms 16:11 RSV).

Even though "we know not the future we know who holds the future in his hand."

Fill in Scriptures

1. _____For which of you desiring to build a tower, does not first sit down and count the cost, whether he has enough to complete it?

2. _____Where there is no vision the people perish (KJV).

3. _____Whoever lacks these things is blind and shortsighted and has forgotten that he has cleansed from his old sins.

4. _____Come now, you who say, 'Today or tomorrow we will go into such and such a town and spend a year there and trade and get gain'; whereas you do not know about tomorrow.

5. _____Remember also your Creator in the days of your youth, before the evil days come, and the years draw nigh when you will say, 'I have no pleasure in them.'

6. _____Prepare to meet your God.

7. _____With her smooth talk she compels him. All at once he follows her, as an ox goes to the slaughter.

8. _____The saying is sure: If we have died with him, we shall also live with him: if we endure, we shall also reign with him; if we deny him, he also will deny us; if we are faithless, he remains faithful—for he cannot deny himself.

9. _____These all died in faith, not having received what was promised, but having seen it and greeted it from afar, and having acknowledged that they were strangers and exiles on the earth.

10. _____And the dust returns to the earth as it was, and the spirit returns to God who gave it.

11. _____Because I have called and you refused to listen . . . and . . . ignored all my counsel . . . I also will laugh at your calamity; I will mock when panic strikes you.

Luke 14:28	Proverbs 1:24-26	Hebrews 11:13
2 Peter 1:9	Ecclesiastes 12:1	2 Timothy 2:11-13
Amos 4:12	James 4:13-14	Ecclesiastes 12:7
Proverbs 7:21-22	Proverbs 29:18 (KJV)	

Questions for Discussion

1. Define foresight.
2. Do you feel this is one of your strong characteristics?
3. Would you wish to be married to or associated in business or other endeavor with someone who had a lack of foresight?
4. How can foresight be a great asset to the church?
5. Explain the lack of foresight as expressed in Luke 12:16-21.
6. What are some obstacles or temptations that stand in the way of foresight?
7. Relate the lack of foresight as expressed in the case of Esau in Genesis 25:29-34.
8. Explain the expression found in James 5:5: "You have fattened hearts in a day of slaughter."
9. Relate the lack of foresight as expressed in the prodigal son in Luke 15:11-19.
10. Name several ways by which one may gain much foresight.
11. Explain the lack of foresight as related in the story found in Luke 16:19-31.
12. Who are the persons most apt to help us gain foresight?
13. How can momentary pleasures, lack of experience and selfishness stand in the way of foresight?
14. Will foresight help us to do all things well?
15. Summarize the need, blessings, and rewards of foresight.

Suggested Assignments

1. Memorize Proverbs 29:18 (KJV); 2 Timothy 2:11-13.
2. Make sentences using the following words: foresight; nearsighted; vision; prudence.
3. Counsel or encourage a sub-teenager to follow Christ with real commitment.

Using Weaknesses in Character as Stepping-Stones to Greatness

Every person has his weak spots in character. It is most important that we be aware of them and face them lest they lead to our defeat. We can actually defeat and make our weaknesses become our assets. Even as Paul said, "When I am weak I am strong." Each person can use his weak points as stepping stones to victory. Character training takes deep interest in what a person lacks. We must all search our hearts for our predominant failing—then learn how to fight against it. Our very first need is then to discover what is worst in us. This is just as important as discovering what is best in us. This can be done in these series of studies. It is vital that we know clearly those weaknesses of character to which we are most frequently tempted.

It is wrong to believe that because we are tempted that we are wicked. James tells us "blessed is the one who endures trial for when he has stood the test he will receive the crown of life" (James 1:12). The blessing is two-fold: it reveals our weak spots in character and gives us opportunity for gaining merit by refusing to surrender to it. Through examination these studies will help reveal our basic defect. Our predominant fault must be dealt with else it will prevail. Some persons are inclined principally to laziness, others to sensuality, anger or materialism, etc. The predominant weak spot may remain hidden to the one possesing it without some kind of training. Weakness in character can be uncovered, brought out in the open and done battle with. No real progress can be made until the master fault is dug up by examination and brought to light.

The secret of character training is to strengthen the weak spots. They must be identified and called by their right and ugly names. The predominate fault will always seek to be covered up in its hiding place to prevent being recognized. "Sometimes the master sin can be detected by discovering what defect makes us most angry when we are accused of it."

Moses used his weakness of character as stepping stones to greatness. "Now the man Moses was very meek" (Numbers 12:3). This was not always his true nature, in fact the very opposite. It was, no doubt, developed through self-examination in character study. He was at one time probably very "hot headed." He killed an Egyptian, in a fit of anger smashed "the tables of stone," and in uncontrolled anger "smote the rock." Here is a man who turned the worst in himself into the best. He became exceedingly meek. Moses fortified the breaches of his soul. They became his strongest points. The Bible is filled with may great saints who have become the very opposite of what they once were.

Let us make the area in life in which we are prone to be defeated the area of our greatest victory. People will say then, I knew him when . . . all to the glory of God.

In dealing with self there are times when we must look for the worst. In dealing with others we must look for the best. Trying to achieve this with prayer, singleness of purpose and study will bring victory.